TRUE POWER

DAVID HEAVENER

TRUE POWER

ACCESS YOUR GOD-GIVEN POWER
AS A CHILD OF GOD

DEFENDER

CRANE, MO

True Power: Access Your God-Given Power as a Child of God
By David Heavener

All rights reserved. Published 2021. Printed in the United States of America.

ISBN: 9781948014472
A CIP catalog record of this book is available from the Library of Congress.

Cover illustration and design by Jeffrey Mardis.

CREED

To my Heavenly Father who gives me His true power.

Contents

Contents

Foreword

We are in the midst of the greatest identity crisis ever seen in America and around the world. For the most part, the people of God have forgotten their power and authority in Christ. This has far-reaching implications. Since the church has relinquished much of its power, it has fallen victim to Satan's attacks.

In Luke 10:19, we learn that Jesus has delegated His power and His authority to His people, all those who are living by faith and trusting in Him:

> Behold, I have given you authority to tread on serpents and scorpions, and overall the power of the enemy, and nothing will injure you.

It's time to rediscover the power of God delegated to you as His son or daughter.

> You will receive power when the Holy Spirit comes on you; and you will be my witnesses in Jerusalem, and in all Judea and Samaria, and to the ends of the earth. (Acts 1:8)

Living each day under the supernatural anointing of the Holy Spirit of God means you will exercise His designated power and authority to defeat the enemy's every strategy, and in doing so, lead others into the same victory.

This book, *True Power*, written by my friend David Heavener, is a blueprint for doing exactly that. The prophet Hosea recorded God saying that His "people perished for lack of knowledge." The same is true today. God's people are suffering defeat because they do not have the biblical knowledge necessary to win each battle. This book will change that. It is a field manual for spiritual warfare.

Read this book, contemplate what David is saying, pray and meditate upon each of the Scriptures presented, and then receive all that God desires for you to have. He has called us to proclaim His excellencies with His power and in His authority.

The true Light of the world is the Lord Jesus Christ. We are to be His instruments to expose and dispel the enemy. We do that through testimony, proclamation, and witness. We have the power to do those things as our birthright. Let's claim that birthright and march forward under the victorious banner of King Jesus.

Pastor Mike Spaulding

Introduction

In these last days, God's children must understand how to use their God-given authority. Jesus said, "Be not deceived; perilous times will come" (Matthew 24:23; 2 Timothy 3:1). The Antichrist is now in full motion, ushering in the one-world government through viruses, lockdowns, cashless society, restrictions, martial law, and more.

Protect Yourself and Your Family

With the principles outlined in God's Word, *True Power* reveals how believers can use their God-given authority and power in the end times. It's of utmost importance that we stand against the enemy of truth, defeating Satan's false teaching as we continue to make disciples who make disciples.

I wrote this book because of the impact one key Scripture verse has had on me:

> You, dear children, are from God and have overcome them, because the one who is in you is greater than the one who is in the world. (1 John 4:4)

If we, as God's elect, don't grasp the truth of this verse, then everything in this book will be diluted, distorted, or even discounted. Though these last days will indeed be extremely difficult, God has not abandoned His people, and He has guaranteed that we will overcome—but we must know how!

True Power connects the truth of God's Word with culture, politics, religion, and relationships, exposing the dark side and exterminating the enemy's agenda for believers. Though God's warriors may experience material success and even abundance, this book is intended solely for spiritual awakening and empowerment. Therefore, we must approach this book as servants craving the Father's truth so we can accomplish heaven's agenda (not our human agenda). This is *not* about finding *our* power. Instead, it's about using the power we have as believers—power that only comes from God, who, in His sovereignty, has given it to His children. This power isn't something we gain on our own, nor can we use it ourselves.

When we exercise God's designated power, the evil one is entirely disabled, though that's also when he makes the most effort to attack. We have the right, power, and authority to do our Creator's work to overcome the enemy and his schemes. The time to start using God's power is *now*.

The modern church is suffering from a power outage; my prayer is that God can use this book to help believers find the switch and turn that power back on.

We need to learn what power is, where it comes from, how to access it, and how to use it properly. The time is short; the harvest is vast. God needs laborers to spread the salvation message, and we need to plug into the power of the Holy Spirit if we are to be competent workers for Christ. Since God is the power source, we are His outlets, transforming the weak and inept into high-powered voltage.

Now that's true power!

True Power

But you will receive power when the Holy Spirit comes on you,
and you will be my witnesses in Jerusalem, and in all Judea
and Samaria, and to the ends of the earth.

ACTS 1:8

True power is the original source, the ultimate dominion, supreme authority. Put simply: True power is God! All other power is lesser than, counterfeit, or a cheap imitation. The real power can only come from the Father. One day that true power was transferred to mankind permanently through Jesus.

> When the crowd saw this, they were filled with awe; and they praised God, who had given such authority to man. (Matthew 9:8)

Just before this verse, we read that Jesus had just healed someone. The religious crowd was upset, but the multitudes marveled. Why? Because they had never seen this kind of authority and power displayed in a man! Throughout Scripture, God demonstrated His power through humans, and He manifested it permanently through His Son Jesus. Because Jesus was God in the flesh, Jesus is power!

However, knowing what power is and understanding how to use it are two separate issues. In these last days, true believers must know how to use our God-given weapon against the enemy. That requires an understanding of authority.

Power Is the Force; Authority Is the "Right" to Use That Force

Power is the weapon and authority is the right to use the weapon. A police officer carries a gun, but it's the badge and the commission that provide the authority to use the weapon. In the same way, we, as children of God, are the only ones authorized to use God's power. We have the authority! In Luke 9:1–2, we read that Jesus called His twelve disciples together and gave them authority over all demons, the power to cast them out, and the power to heal all diseases. It was only at this point in history that God gave His people the right to use the same power He possesses.

If power is the gun, then truth is the ammo, and authority pulls the trigger!

We Are the Authority!

In most states in America and other countries, we must have a permit to carry a firearm. Why? Because in the hands of an untrained person, or an evil person, the gun can be used as a deadly weapon to harm an innocent victim.

Every person who uses God's true power must first be vetted and trained to use it properly.

1. **Vetted.** We need to understand that we are God's property. We're abiding in and by His love for us. Being a child of God means we belong

to Him. When we truly abide in Him, we're willing to risk everything for Him. It is only by being a child of God that we have access to His power.

2. **Trained.** We often send children to school for seven hours a day to learn reading, writing, and arithmetic, but we spend a small fraction of that time, or none at all, teaching them the Word of God. If they hear God's Word preached, it's rarely with power and authority. Second Timothy 2:15 says:

> Do your best to present yourself to God as one approved, a worker who does not need to be ashamed and who correctly handles the word of truth.

Let's start training the Body of Christ by reading and understanding the real meaning of Scripture. I don't mean listening to a thirty-minute Sunday school lesson taken out of a mass-printed book that's written and published according to a denominational agenda. We need to take a hard, honest look at the Word of God regarding power and authority.

In the King James translation of the Bible, the word "power" appears 118 times in the Old Testament and 121 times in the New Testament. The *Oxford Dictionary on Lexicon* defines "power" as "the capacity or ability to direct or influence others' behavior or the course of events, possession of control, authority or influence over others, a physical might." We read that God told Moses in Exodus 9:16:

> But I have raised you up for this very purpose, that I might show you power and that my name might be proclaimed in all the earth.

God displayed His power by bringing the plagues upon Egypt. Moses spoke of this power in Exodus 15:6:

Your right hand, Lord, was majestic in power. Your right hand, Lord, shattered the enemy.

King David said:

It is God who arms me with strength and keeps my way secure. (2 Samuel 22:33)

David knew the source of his power to accomplish mighty things. God controls the wind by His power, as mentioned in Psalm 78:26. The disciples commented on this power in Matthew 8:27:

The men were amazed and asked, "What kind of man is this? Even the winds and the waves obey him!"

But little ol' us? How can we have God's power? Fortunately, neither our size, gender, race, education, fame, fortune, nor anything else ever determines God's power.

The prophet Isaiah said:

He gives strength to the weary and increases the power of the weak. (Isaiah 40:29)

God gives power to the weak. He loves to be countercultural and use the underdogs, the misfits, and the unwanted to magnify His amazing power.

Bullies, Meet God's Power

From grades six through ten, I was small for my age, I wore glasses, I was heavy, and I was so unpopular that I don't believe anyone ever really saw me, except when they wanted to pick on me. They bullied me to the point that I had a knot in my stomach every school morning. I always hoped I wouldn't get beaten up too badly.

Fortunately, my parents had always taken me to church, where I learned to pray. So, pray I did—not only after school but during class, even to the point that the other kids made fun of me when I closed my eyes. However, through my prayers, God's power began to manifest in several ways:

1. I had peace. The knot in my stomach disappeared.
2. I became bolder. I looked the bullies in the eyes, and they knew my fear wasn't paralyzing me any longer.
3. I took action. I no longer ran the other way, but I stayed my course toward the classroom. If they were in my way, I didn't turn back.

When we walk in God's true power, we disarm the devil! Through prayer, I was able to experience this power firsthand!

A Soldier Understood Power and Authority

Three Greek words are used in the Bible for "power":

dunamis—"miraculous power"
kratos—"dominion or ruling power"
exousia—"authority and influence"

We often put power and authority in the same bucket and think they have the same meaning and purpose, but let's look a little deeper at the Scripture application. Matthew 8:5–10 gives us this account:

When Jesus had entered Capernaum, a centurion came to him, asking for help. "Lord," he said, "my servant lies at home paralyzed, suffering terribly." Jesus said to him, "Shall I come and heal him?" The centurion replied, "Lord, I do not deserve to have you come under my roof. But just say the word, and my servant will be healed. For I myself am a man under authority, with soldiers under me. I tell this one, 'Go,' and he goes; and that one, 'Come,' and he comes. I say to my servant, 'Do this,' and he does it." When Jesus heard this, he was amazed and said to those following him, "Truly I tell you, I have not found anyone in Israel with such great faith."

When the centurion went to Jesus and asked Him to heal his servant, the powerful man realized that Jesus didn't have to come to his house; he understood the authority Jesus possessed and what it means to have authority. The soldier was a commander, a chief, the head of his regime. He could simply speak the command and it would be done.

Why? Because he was in a position of authority! This centurion applied the same analogy to Jesus and His kingdom as he did to the Roman military—which certainly astonished our Lord, because the centurion was not a Jew. He most likely knew little, if anything, about the Torah and Jewish law. However, he did know something that few others in all of Israel understood: authority and how to apply it!

To Possess Power, We Must Understand Authority

Most commentaries fail to understand how to interpret what the soldier said before explaining the meaning of authority to Christ. He said, "I am not worthy of having you come into my house." The soldier knew Christ was a unique person who possessed supernatural abilities because of His reputation of being able to heal. However, what the soldier meant was not that he, the soldier, was inferior (though I believe he understood that). He indicated that he didn't have the authority Jesus had. The soldier knew Jesus had a commission given only to Him—by Someone in a higher position.

I believe this centurion knew Jesus was from God. When Jesus declared to His followers that He had not found this kind of "faith" in all of Israel, He wasn't speaking only to the fact that the centurion admitted he was inferior to Jesus. Jesus said the man understood and proclaimed the truth regarding the authority to use God's power.

The New Testament says Jesus gave power and authority to His disciples. Where did the power and authority come from for all the miracles, healings, and supernatural events until that time? Didn't God's people already have authority?

The answer is no. They only had limited access to God's power. It was the same power with the same effects, but they were limited in their use of it. God had to be with them, and He had to have ordained it. Why? Because God had not yet sent the Holy Spirit.

The difference between God's people now and the heroes of yesterday is Jesus, His blood, His death, and His resurrection. Christ and what He did for us changed everything regarding authority and power.

If you own a concealed weapon permit, you have specific rights to carry a gun, but you're limited regarding the kind of weapon you can carry. How you carry it and for how long depends on the expiration date of your permit. However, in God's kingdom, we don't need a permit to use God's power; we already carry the authority to use His power. It's unlimited, and it will never expire. We can pray "in the name of Jesus." The name of our Savior gives us continuous authority.

In John 16:23 and John 14:12–14, Jesus told His disciples to no longer ask Him for anything; instead, He said, they should go directly to the Father and "ask in my [Jesus'] name." Jesus passed on to His people the authority and exclusive right to use God's power—*kratos*—

dominion or ruling power. God first gave dominion to Adam and Eve in the Garden of Eden, as detailed in Genesis 1:26. We will get further into that in the next chapter, but mankind lost that right due to sin, and the devil became the "god of this world." The great news is that when we repent and receive Christ and His sacrifice, we experience the new birth, and we can take back our *kratos* power.

John 1:12 states:

> Yet to all who did receive him, to those who believed in his name,
> he gave the *right* to become children of God. (emphasis added)

Again the Greek word translated as "right" is *kratos*: Our Lord gave back dominion and rule to believers.

Two Powers: Which Will You Choose?

The Greek word *exousia* describes authority or influential power. Every person, saved or unsaved, is under the *exousia*—the spiritual influence and authority of the devil or God. The Apostle Paul said in his letter to the Ephesians (2:1–2) that they lived in disobedience when they "followed the ways of this world and of the ruler of the kingdom of the air." However, he quickly added that "the spirit…is now at work in those who are disobedient." When we receive Christ as Lord and Savior, He delivers us from the power (*exousia*) of darkness. This truth is made known in Colossians 1:13:

> For he has rescued us from the dominion of darkness and
> brought us into the kingdom of the Son he loves.

Jesus freed us from the influence and the authority of Satan, and God, the Father, expects us to operate in His power (*exousia*). Jesus preached the Word of God with *exousia*——authority.

We Overcome Only with God's Power

Luke 4:31–32 states:

> Then he went down to Capernaum, a town in Galilee, and on the Sabbath he taught the people. They were amazed at his teaching because his words had authority.

The early disciples preached the Word of God in *exousia*—authority. First Thessalonians 1:5 says:

> Our gospel came to you not simply with words but also with power, with the Holy Spirit and deep conviction. You know how we lived among you for your sake.

Jesus has given us the same *exousia* authority He and the early disciples had. This promise is in Luke 10:19 (KJV):

> Behold, I give unto you power [*exousia*] to tread on serpents and scorpions, and over all the power [*dunamis*] of the enemy: and nothing shall by any means hurt you.

Notice the first part of Jesus' promise says He gives us the "power to tread on serpents and scorpions" (these creatures represent the enemy). The Greek word used here is *exousia*: God gives authority to us. In the second part of the promise, the word "power" is translated from the Greek word *dunamis*. This means that all the miraculous, supernatural power over the enemy falls under our authority.

We have the *dunamis* ("miraculous power"), the *kratos* ("dominion and ruling power"), and the *exousia* ("authority power") in Jesus' name to defeat the enemy.

Now that's true power.

The Origin of Power

I lift up my eyes to the mountains—
where does my help come from? My help comes
from the Lord, the Maker of heaven and earth.
PSALM 121:1–2

In order to utilize our God-given power, we must understand where it originates. The obvious answer is from God, but how did it get here on earth? The prophet Jeremiah gives insight:

> But God made the earth by his power; he founded the world by his wisdom and stretched out the heavens by his understanding. (Jeremiah 10:12)

Power comes from the Creator; God is the source of true power. The power has always existed; however, we see in Genesis that this was the introduction of God's power into our dimension—the dimension of time on earth. Genesis 1:26 states:

> Then God said, "Let us make mankind in our image, in our likeness, so that they may rule over the fish in the sea and the

birds in the sky, over the livestock and all the wild animals, and over all the creatures that move along the ground."

Mankind wasn't only made in the Creator's image, but was also given dominion over all the earth. God granted Adam and Eve authority and power. He had given the first couple a beautiful garden and the whole earth to rule as king and queen. The animals and nature itself were their subjects.

The Power Grab

However, one of God's other creations sought power and authority for himself. Lucifer, the anointed cherub of God, held the highest position of the angels in heaven and was perfect before evil crept into his heart. We find this stated in Ezekiel 28:15:

> You were blameless in your ways from the day you were created
> till wickedness was found in you.

When Lucifer's beauty and wisdom led him to the prideful assumption that he could ascend above the Most High, then God had to strip Lucifer of his authority; He cast him from the holy mountain of God to earth.

Lucifer lost his position and his authority in heaven, and his name, which means "light-bringer," was changed to "Satan," which means "adversary." He became an enemy of God. Lucifer is also referred to by many other names throughout Scripture, including "serpent," "dragon," and the "prince of the power of the air."

The name "Satan" is fitting, given that he is the adversary of our faith. Satan was defeated and banished from the eternal kingdom; however, he pursued a new conquest in his humiliation and pride. He set his sights on seizing the rule that belonged to God's children, Adam and Eve.

The Enemy's Plot

The fallen angel's plot was to separate God's children from Creator God by breaking the relationship and forever alienating the children's connection to the eternal kingdom. Satan was strategic; he came as a serpent and deceived mankind by convincing them to disobey the Creator:

> Now the serpent was more crafty than any of the wild animals the Lord God had made. He said to the woman, "Did God really say, 'You must not eat from any tree in the garden'?"
>
> The woman said to the serpent, "We may eat fruit from the trees in the garden, but God did say, 'You must not eat fruit from the tree that is in the middle of the garden, and you must not touch it, or you will die.'"
>
> "You will not certainly die," the serpent said to the woman. "For God knows that when you eat from it your eyes will be opened, and you will be like God, knowing good and evil." (Genesis 3:1–5)

Adam and Eve Forfeited Their Power

The first couple did partake of the fruit, thus they committed high treason against their Creator. This act bore a spirit of independence and rebellion. God's offspring had now joined the ranks of Satan, the Creator's arch enemy. The first couple were stripped of their titles and forfeited their dominion over the earth to Satan.

Adam and Eve were banished from the garden and lost their connection to Creator God and His Spirit. As a result of their actions, mankind would no longer be able to see things from a spiritual perspective. Instead, humans would view things from a physical standpoint, which is extremely limiting and leads to confusion. Satan's rule started to take over the earth, bringing darkness and malevolence.

Satan was able to take power and authority from Adam and Eve, but that doesn't mean he has full control of the world. It was God who permitted Satan to have that control after Adam and Eve sinned. God always maintains authority; Satan can only do what God ordains.

Satan Meets His Match

Luke 4:5–6 says:

> The devil led him up to a high place and showed him in an instant all the kingdoms of the world. And he said to him, "I will give you all their authority and splendor; it has been given to me, and I can give it to anyone I want to."

Who delivered that power to Satan? We know it could only come from God, and since Christ is God's Son, Satan was playing a power game with God in that desert. Unfortunately for Satan, God's wisdom is more than a match for the evil one.

Matthew 28:18 confirms this:

> Then Jesus came to them and said, "All authority in heaven and on earth has been given to me."

The demons and unclean spirits knew this and trembled in Jesus' presence. Mark 3:11 states:

Whenever the impure spirits saw him, they fell down before him and cried out, "You are the Son of God."

When Jesus left the earth, He transferred that authority to us—you and I, His children. Matthew 10:1 explains the power given to all of Christ's followers:

Jesus called his twelve disciples to him and gave them authority to drive out impure spirits and to heal every disease and sickness.

That's power! As stated earlier, God gave power to Adam, who misused it and lost it. This may be confusing, because we have learned that Satan reigns over this earth. But remember, God cast him out of heaven. Rule over an earthly kingdom and authority in the spiritual realm are two different paradigms.

In summary, God is the origin of power. He gave His power to man, who lost it to Satan. God gives His children a second chance to regain the power through His Son, Jesus—and now the war is raging.

The earth is a battleground, with the two powers at odds. Satan's power is a poor reflection of God's; it's been manipulated and perverted. The only true source of power—real power—is God. He is its origin. Demons are merely counterfeit; they are deceiving with false gospels and lying signs and wonders in these last days.

You and I are warriors in God's army. It's time to armor up! Grasp your power and move forward in this battle that we will win. Greater is He who is in us than that snake that's in the world.

3

Power War

For we wrestle not against flesh and blood, but against
principalities, against powers, against the rulers of the darkness
of this world, against spiritual wickedness in high places.

EPHESIANS 6:12, KJV

In order to even declare war over power, we must first understand that God's power is not the *only* power!

Until we grasp the fact that we are soldiers in God's army and need to prepare for battle, we will continue to be sick, weak, and useless to the Body of Christ. Unfortunately, most modern-day churches don't preach real spiritual warfare; they only present the make-believe kind. Oh yes, they quote Scripture passages addressing the topic of "we battle not against flesh and blood" and sing songs about being in "God's army," but they never get in the foxhole. In fact, about the time the bombs start dropping and bullets start flying, their one-and-only weekly church service is over, and they're all pigging out at their favorite restaurants.

Know Your Enemy!

Any military person will tell you that one of the most important aspects of war is to know the enemy. I remember playing football as a younger man; the coach had us watch videos and study the other teams' tactics on the field so that we would learn their moves. The Bible reveals the enemy's origin, agenda, and tactics against God's people. Let's take a look at the hierarchy of evil, the commander and chief of hell himself—Satan.

God Has an Army; So Does Satan!

You can't have a war if there aren't two opposing forces, two armies. Satan has a fleet of minions roaming the earth "seeking whom they may devour," and, boy, are they having a feast on many unaware and ill-equipped Christians. Satan's evil minions are behind every addiction, illness, perversion, family collapse, and financial problem, as well as behind every kind of plague that comes against God's children. Earlier, we discovered that Christ possessed God's power; now let's see how He used it. Our Lord's first recorded encounter with Satan was at the beginning of His ministry, and it took place in the desert right after His forty-day fast. This account is found in Matthew 4:1–11—a passage of Scripture that's often called "the temptation of Christ," but that I like to call "God's first punch" because it's when Jesus gave His first command to the devil (in verse 10):

> Jesus said to him, "Away from me, Satan! For it is written: 'Worship the Lord your God, and serve him only.'"

Basically, Satan tried to seduce Christ three times, offering Him anything under the sun. Satan's strategy was to take Scripture out of context, but the last time he did so, Jesus was finally fed up and cast him out—using Scripture to do it!

Does Satan Go To Church?

After that, the first place where Jesus encountered a demon was in a synagogue!

> And in the synagogue there was a man, which had a spirit of an unclean devil, and cried out with a loud voice, saying, "Let us alone; what have we to do with thee, thou Jesus of Nazareth? art thou come to destroy us? I know thee who thou art; the Holy One of God."
>
> And Jesus rebuked him, saying, "Hold thy peace, and come out of him. And when the devil had thrown him in the midst, he came out of him, and hurt him not." (Luke 4:33–35, KJV)

So what's a demon doing in the house of God today? He's using a twisted version of Scripture to build his one-world religious system through diversion and deception.

A New Marshal in Town

When I was a kid, I watched *Gunsmoke* with my dad. I couldn't wait for Marshal Dillon to show up and bring justice to all the bad guys in Dodge City. Every time I read a Scripture passage about our Lord dealing with demons, I just can't help but think of how Dodge City was the most evil town on the planet, running rampant with cowboys who had no respect for the law. In the same way, demons not only have no respect for God's law, but they hate it. And if you're a true, born-again child of God, they hate you, too.

But we know now that we have the power of the Living God in us—the same power Jesus displayed in Capernaum. When we use that power, the demons tremble, just like they did when they saw Jesus.

And unclean spirits, when they saw him (Jesus), fell down before him, and cried, saying, "Thou art the Son of God." (Mark 3:11)

Today, when a child of God nears a demon, the effect should be the same: Demons tremble, demons shake, and demons obey!

The seventy-two returned with joy and said, "Lord, even the demons submit to us in your name!" (Luke 10:17)

It is that name, and that name alone, that wins the power war.

Power Transfer

That power is the same as the mighty strength he
exerted when he raised Christ from the dead and
seated him at his right hand in the heavenly realms.

EPHESIANS 1:19–20

In Matthew 24, our Lord precisely details what will happen before He returns. The Antichrist will be in full-blown motion; however, he must overcome to rule. Do you remember the verse that tells us "greater is He who is in me than he who is in the world" (1 John 4:4)? If we don't use the power that Christ transferred to us, then that power can default to the enemy.

When God cast Satan from heaven, He gave Satan power on earth; therefore, Satan has dominion over the earth. When God sent His Son into the world, Satan knew his power took second place, because Jesus gave us power to overcome the evil one. So, there are two powers in play: God's and Satan's. If true believers don't know how to use their power in these last days, then the enemy will have a field day.

Scripture tells us the demons trembled and bowed to Jesus because God's authority has dominion over all and rules over everything. But how and when was the power of Christ transferred? Before He suffered and died on the cross and left this world, He promised us that the Comforter, the Holy Spirit, would come:

> But you will receive power when the Holy Spirit comes on you;
> you will be my witnesses in Jerusalem, and in all Judea and
> Samaria, and to the ends of the earth. (Acts 1:8)

The "you" in this verse refers not only to the disciples, but also to you and me personally. Most think the Comforter is only here to console us, make things cozy and soft, and make everything feel good, but that's not the case. In fact, the Bible doesn't promise a warm, fuzzy life to believers at all.

The Holy Spirit is supernatural power manifested in the natural, and this power is no match for the evil one. This was the original transfer of power from God to man, through His Son, Jesus Christ, by way of the Holy Spirit. Even though many men and women have possessed God's power and displayed incredible miracles, it's the first time God's power can now live inside us continually.

Take Comfort

> But the Comforter, which is the Holy Ghost, whom the Father
> will send in my name, he shall teach you all things, and bring all
> things to your remembrance, whatsoever I have said unto you.
> (John 14:26, KJV)

It's essential to understand what the word "Comforter" means here. The Greek word used here for it is *parakletos*, an "advocate," an "intercessor," a "consoler," a "comforter," and a "helper." In the broadest sense, the Holy Spirit takes the place of Christ on earth to equip believers in spiritual warfare, evicting demons, healing the sick, and raising the dead.

Sometimes we get caught up in the acts of demon warfare and healing and we forget that wisdom is the most crucial aspect of power. What good is it to have a weapon if we don't know how to use it?

Simply stated, the Comforter empowers us in every aspect of the spiritual realm. Satan has no rule over us, because the power transferred to us is the original and ultimate power—the same power that raised Christ from the dead:

> And if the Spirit of him who raised Jesus from the dead is living in you, he who raised Christ from the dead will also give life to your mortal bodies because of his Spirit who lives in you. (Romans 8:11)

Now that is power!

The battle is in full force, the enemy has ramped up his attacks, and the clock is ticking. It's time for God's elect to stand up, take authority, and use the power that Christ gave us when He left this earth. Until we do, the apostate church and its counterfeit religion will continue having a field day with Satan's influence.

Since we have established that there are two separate powers, which will you choose? If you base your answer on the fact that you belong to a particular denomination, you're in for a fall—and a hard one!

Just like Jesus fought the demons of the religious system, we battle the same demons in a more ramped-up version as we enter these last days. The Antichrist is in full swing. In fact, we must understand that he and the false prophets are already working through the modern-day religious system.

Ladies and gentlemen, introducing the modern-day deception Christ spoke about in Matthew 24:

> Jesus answered: "Watch out that no one deceives you. For many will come in my name, claiming, 'I am the Messiah,' and will deceive many." (Matthew 24:4–5)

Satan is deceiving in these last days, and if a believer can't identify the deception, how is it possible to identify the true power?

Did God Become Man So That Man Could Become God?

This may sound like some statement by the Dalai Lama spewing New-Age rhetoric, but, unfortunately, it's the central theme of most of today's churches. Whether or not they admit it, they have traded the truth and the real Jesus for a "Candyland Jesus"—one who is at their beck and call, who's there to serve them, and who will bring them abundance in this life, whether it's through more money, a better job, a classier car, or anything else that boosts and motivates their lifestyle in a way that seems beautiful to the world, but is disgusting to God. They are using power, but it's the power of the Antichrist! This power from Satan is the deceptive power Christ speaks of in Matthew 24: "and many false prophets will appear and deceive many people" (Matthew 24:11).

But, praise God, this power can never stand up to God's true power. Christ says that many will choose the Antichrist's power, and because of their love of self and sin, their love will grow cold.

> Because of the increase of wickedness, the love of most will grow cold. (Matthew 24:12)

The remnant hasn't grown cold, but they certainly haven't yet fully awakened. That, however, is about to change as we approach the fulfillment of end-times prophecy. Now that the battle lines are drawn and sides are being chosen, get ready for the power war.

Training for Service

So, what's the next step after accepting our position in God's army? It's one thing to enlist, but another to start training.

First, we study and know God's character by understanding His Word. God's Word isn't merely what we see written; it's the force behind it—the power.

> For the kingdom of God is not a matter of talk but of power.
> (1 Corinthians 4:20)

God backs every instruction with power. But, believer, beware! Even though Scripture is "God-breathed," it's also used by Satan, such as when Christ encountered the evil one in the desert. As we discussed earlier, Satan tried to manipulate Jesus by quoting Scripture; even though Satan used God's words, he used them corruptly in an effort to trick Jesus into sinning, like the Antichrist is manipulating God's signs and wonders today. Addressing the religious community in Matthew 22:29, "Jesus replied, 'You are in error because you do not know the Scriptures or the power of God.'"

Studying Scripture without using God's power is like firing a gun with no bullets; you can pull the trigger as many times as you like and be a great marksman, but without the ammunition of God's power, you'll never take out the enemy.

> Finally, be strong in the Lord and in his mighty power. Put on
> the full armor of God, so that you can take your stand against
> the devil's schemes. (Ephesians 6:10–11)

The war is raging, and the question remains: Which side will you choose? It's your choice and your destiny, eternally.

5

Power Creates Enemies

Then you will be handed over to be persecuted and put to
death, and you will be hated by all nations because of me.

MATTHEW 24:9

A friend of mine, a well-known movie producer, was heading to court to defend himself in a significant legal battle. I asked him if he had lost sleep because of the stress of the lawsuit. He answered: "Not at all. It's a confirmation of my success. Unless you have something of great value that someone wants, then you have nothing at all!"

We have something the world doesn't: We have power. God's power is in us. We're a danger to Satan, and he wants to cripple us in his courts of hell.

Anytime we step out of the norm, we run the risk of creating enemies, especially when we're filled with the Holy Spirit. Why? It depends on whether we're encountering the unchurched or the apostate church. Let's look at the most destructive: the apostate church.

Religion has a man-made agenda with a whole bunch of baggage. Some religions are very strict, and some aren't. Therefore, we might get away with certain actions or behaviors in one church but not in another. But in any case, when we go against some doctrine and tradition, we could be facing an emotional and spiritual hurricane.

When the Lord tells us to say or do something for Him, it may seem illogical, impractical, or even impossible. When we obey God's voice and go against the crowd, whether to befriend someone caught in sin or go someplace where we'll meet opposition, it is vital to be led by the Spirit to speak up for truth and stand up for God.

Maybe we'll be called to help someone at a time that seems to be inconvenient or inappropriate. This is what happened to Jesus, as we read in Mark 3:1–6:

> Another time Jesus went into the synagogue, and a man with a shriveled hand was there. Some of them were looking for a reason to accuse Jesus, so they watched him closely to see if he would heal him on the Sabbath. Jesus said to the man with the shriveled hand, "Stand up in front of everyone." Then Jesus asked them, "Which is lawful on the Sabbath: to do good or to do evil, to save life or to kill?" But they remained silent. He looked around at them in anger and, deeply distressed at their stubborn hearts, said to the man, "Stretch out your hand." He stretched it out, and his hand was completely restored. Then the Pharisees went out and began to plot with the Herodians how they might kill Jesus.

While He was in Capernaum, Jesus went to the synagogue and noticed a man there with a deformed hand. Since it was the Sabbath, Jesus' enemies were watching Him closely. Would He heal the man's hand, breaking the Law regarding what one can and cannot do on the Sabbath? If He did, they planned to arrest Him!

Notice here that Jesus was entering a synagogue, a place "set apart" for God—for worship and teaching. Yet it was the right setting for a spiritual battle between the forces of good and evil, love and hate. It was the Sabbath day, "set apart" by God for people to show their love and respect for Him. The important thing the Pharisees were missing was that Jesus is God, the Lord of the Sabbath. Matthew 12:8 confirms this truth:

For the Son of Man is Lord even of the Sabbath day.

On that Sabbath day, like on many other days, Jesus spotted someone with a need. He saw a man who most likely had been waiting, hoping Jesus would heal him. The religious Pharisees were watching to see what Christ was going to do, because they knew His thoughts and actions were always about love, kindness, compassion, and healing. But their thoughts were hateful, self-centered, and destructive—the opposite of Christ's.

Where the True Test Begins

As stated earlier, if Jesus were to heal the man on the Sabbath, His enemies could have Him arrested for breaking the Law. But Jesus wasn't worried about what the Pharisees thought. Instead, He had compassion for the man.

In the Mark 3 passage, the Pharisees wouldn't answer Jesus' questions, which brought the truth to light. Then, Jesus looked at the Pharisees angrily, because He was deeply disturbed by their indifference to human need.

Where the Decision Is Made

After Jesus healed the man, He was hurt and furious about the condition of the Pharisees' hearts, which were callused toward those in need. Jesus had no problem deciding what to do; since He was God, He didn't tolerate their sin or their lack of mercy, and He healed the man's hand.

Don't Play God!

Notice that Jesus didn't place any restrictions or conditions on the man; He simply healed him because there was a need. When we meet someone whom God has called us to help, we shouldn't ask them if they are Christians, go to church, drink or use drugs, or ask them anything about their past. We should simply meet their needs right where they are.

If the Holy Spirit permits, we can get into the spiritual aspect of their lives. Too often, we're called by God to use our power to meet physical needs, but instead, we try to delve into their spiritual condition first. God doesn't always ask us to do that. Many times, He calls us to try to meet spiritual needs after we plant the seed of helping with the physical needs.

Once God reveals His power to the religious world, watch out! Here comes the hell-storm!

Enemies Will Unite!

Returning to the conclusion of the Mark 3 passage, after Jesus had healed the man and likely after noting His anger at them, the Pharisees immediately went away and met with the Herodians to discuss plans for killing Jesus. Isn't it interesting that the same Pharisees who were condemning Jesus for healing on the Sabbath were plotting to kill Him?

When our enemies come against us, they usually go to our other adversaries for assistance, which we see happening here. Before this time, the Pharisees and the Herodians were enemies. But here, they joined forces to come against Christ simply because they had the same agenda: Kill Jesus!

Jesus didn't let these evil men stop His mission. We won't allow united enemies to stop us either, no matter the consequences. We need to listen to the Holy Spirit, use the power we're given, and act upon His instruction with the promise that He will guide and comfort us. Jesus warned us, in John 15:18–21, that there would be those who hate us:

> If the world hates you, keep in mind that it hated me first. If you belonged to the world, it would love you as its own. As it is, you do not belong to the world, but I have chosen you out of the world. That is why the world hates you. Remember what I told you: "A servant is not greater than his master." If they persecuted me, they would persecute you also. If they obeyed my teaching, they would obey yours also. They will treat you this way because of my name, for they do not know the one who sent me.

Satan is the leader of the band of demonic forces who are hellbent on thwarting God's objectives. But, rest assured: There is good news, brothers, and sisters. Jesus tells us that the plans of the enemy will fail.

> They triumphed over him by the blood of the Lamb and by the word of their testimony; they did not love their lives so much as to shrink from death. (Revelation 12:11)

So, we must remember, even though following Christ will create enemies, we are overcomers. Our word is most powerful as we proclaim the Living God who gives us true power!

6

Power's Greatest Enemy

When the Sabbath came, he began to teach in the synagogue,
and many who heard him were amazed. "Where did this man
get these things?" they asked. "What's this wisdom that has been
given him? What are these remarkable miracles he is performing?
Isn't this the carpenter? Isn't this Mary's son and the brother of
James, Joseph, Judas, and Simon? Aren't his sisters here with us?"
And they took offense at him.

MARK 6:2–3

This is a hard chapter for me to write. I envision our Lord coming
home to teach, heal, cast out demons, and serve His own family. If
that were me, I imagine how excited I would be to help my city, community, family, and friends. This visit, however, did not go well. The community shunned Him. They couldn't see the power of God He possessed,
because they saw only the youth who had grown up in their town.

Jesus said to them, "A prophet is not without honor except in his
own town, among his relatives and in his own home." (Mark 6:4)

As a songwriter and then an actor/filmmaker, I remember traveling to various cities to promote my new CD or latest film. Press and fans showed considerable enthusiasm and encouragement. But, when I'd go back to my hometown and visit people I've known all my life, I felt like I was on a different planet. Very few showed interest in my songs or films like the rest of the world had. I remember asking my close friend, "Why don't my people show enthusiasm like people I don't know?" He replied, "David, it's because they only remember you for who you were, not who you are now."

Wow! That hit home, because since I've been on this "truth tour" for God, I notice it again: When I'm around people who knew me then, they don't see who I am now. I am a child of the Living God, a faithful follower of Christ carrying the power as He did. Why, then, is the power of God not manifest when I'm around family and friends?

> He could not do any miracles there, except lay his hands on a few sick people and heal them. He was amazed at their lack of faith. (Mark 6:5–6)

Unbelief is the absence or lack of faith. Unbelief is the enemy of God. If we are devoid of faith, then we have *no power*. Jesus stated to the woman with the twelve-year bleeding issue in Mark 5:25–34, "Your faith has made you whole." Unfortunately, unbelief can happen even to God's people at various times in our striving to be all the Father wants us to be. Therefore, it is of utmost importance to be on guard against unbelief, which is power's greatest enemy. This—unbelief—is also the reason for God's deepest heartache concerning His people.

> And without faith, it is impossible to please God because anyone who comes to him must believe that he exists and that he rewards those who earnestly seek him. (Hebrews 11:6)

Faith equals power. Through faith, God manifests the reward in us. But why is our reward, for the most part, disconnected from those who are close to us? Have your family and friends given you pushback about your faith? Do they ignore you or come against you, calling you radical or even crazy? If they haven't, they are either like-minded, very tolerant, or you are not using God's power in the way He intends. Search your heart regarding where you stand with God and His power.

There could have been several reasons Jesus' community, friends, and family didn't team with Him. If this has happened to you, explore the specifics of why your family and friends have shunned you. Let's look at a few primary reasons for rejection:

1. Jesus used His power.
2. People weren't looking at the supernatural aspect of Christ's actions.
3. People were jealous.
4. People were fearful.

Jesus Used His Power

If He had never healed, cast out demons, or taught with words of authority, no one would have a reason to come against Jesus. But He did, and we have that same power in us. So why would we expect people to treat us any differently than they do Christ?

> If the world hates you, keep in mind that it hated me first. If you belonged to the world, it would love you as its own. As it is, you do not belong to the world, but I have chosen you out of the world. That is why the world hates you. (John 15:18–19)

People Weren't Looking at the Supernatural Aspect of Christ's Actions

Mark 6:3 says:

> "Isn't this the carpenter? Isn't this Mary's son and the brother of James, Joseph, Judas, and Simon? Aren't his sisters here with us?" And they took offense at him.

This verse clearly shows that Jesus' hometown friends and family were only looking at Him in the flesh. They had watched Him grow up—running around as a boy, playing games, and doing the things children do. This could be how your family and friends see you; they may still view you as a child, playing silly games and making foolish mistakes. Most are not looking at your new nature, only at your old, carnal self. When we are saved, our former selves die. Christ sees a new creation in us, but the people around us struggle to come to terms with this concept, seeing us as who we were in the past.

People Were Jealous

"Misery loves company." This expression reminds me of country songs about people crying into their beer and lingering around others doing the same. Why? Because in many situations, most people—especially our family and friends—don't want us to outdo them; maybe they feel this way because it makes them look at the limitations of their own life. Or, perhaps they don't want to be left alone to cry into their beer of unbelief. Perhaps Jesus' family didn't want Him to be any different from what they remembered Him to be: a boy and a child. It's plain to see that they were aware of His power and its reality.

Even though your family and friends may witness your power by your words or actions, they may not understand it or process it because they're not connected to the truth. Only truth can connect a soul to the supernatural. Christ experienced this, and He said we would also.

> When the Sabbath came, he began to teach in the synagogue, and many who heard him were amazed. "Where did this man get these things?" they asked. "What's this wisdom that has been given him? What are these remarkable miracles he is performing?" (Mark 6:2)

Jesus' friends and family had the proof and evidence of His power, yet they couldn't yield to the truth. If your family or friends have seen the truth and the power of God, yet continue to turn a blind eye to God's real authority, it's because they don't want you to rise above their position in their religion.

Yes, I did say "religion," not "relationship." A relationship with God thrusts us forward, but religion always holds us back. Most people in the church are very comfortable right where they are: same church, same pew, same sermon, and same routine—week after week. This is their god. They don't want to see the power of God manifested, because it may expose their lukewarm condition.

People Were Fearful

Since the crowd in Jesus' hometown was very traditional and religious, they held their position, because stepping "out of the box" could have been detrimental to their lifestyle. Jesus' reputation was that He came with power. Thus, religious sectors hated Him.

The religious people wanted to hold onto their power, which was not God's power. It could be that your family and friends don't want to be an outcast like you. They don't want to be considered radical, weird, or even dangerous. They don't want to go through what they're putting you through; they may even abandon you because of their rejection.

We might think that the enemy of power is rejection. Rejection is a result of the real enemy: unbelief. It breaks my heart to think about how God in the flesh must have felt when He came home to such unbelief. But the tragedy was when those who appeared to be close to Him abandoned Him, watching Him being crucified by the enemy of God: unbelief.

Power's Best Friend: Protection

*But the Lord is faithful, and he will strengthen
you and protect you from the evil one.*

2 THESSALONIANS 3:3

At least twenty of the fifty films I've made were action films that always had fight scenes; many involved hand-to-hand combat using various martial arts and street-fighting tactics. In every such scene, one truth prevails: A good fighter is always an expert at defense. To win a battle, one must be better at *protecting* than at *projecting*. During fight scenes, the "good guy" is always blocking the enemy's potentially fatal blows—until that one opportunity arises for the protagonist to use a unique weapon to destroy the antagonist.

In his letter to the Ephesians, Paul shared some of these same principles. In fact, Ephesians 6:13–18 says we should put on the "full armor" of God. "Armor" (Greek: *panoplia*, "full armor") is defined as "a protective covering."

Most readers are familiar with the Ephesians verse cited above about our fight not being against "flesh and blood," but against "principalities, against powers, and the rulers of the darkness." However, this verse is sandwiched between others that give specific instructions on combating—and defeating—the enemy.

> Finally, be strong in the Lord and in his mighty power. Put on the full armor of God, so that you can take your stand against the devil's schemes. (Ephesians 6:10–11)

Here, we're told to strap on God's armor so that we can survive the enemy's assaults; however, our actions are considered to be offensive moves. In other words, we may have learned that putting on God's armor is all about moving forward and battling the enemy. But, in reality, it's all about *protection*.

> Therefore put on the full armor of God, so that when the day of evil comes, you may be able to stand your ground, and after you have done everything, to stand. (Ephesians 6:13)

Many well-meaning Christians are out there fighting a losing battle with the enemy because they remain on the offense, thinking that this is how God intends us to deal with the evil one. To my knowledge, Jesus never sought out an encounter with a demon; instead, when they manifested, He dealt with them. Christ even went out of His way to avoid evil; He miraculously passed through the angry crowd of people who were trying to kill him in His hometown of Nazareth (see Luke 4:28–30).

In Ephesians 6:10, we learn that God is backing us with *kratos* power: the full ruling power of His might! Then, the next verse (Ephesians 6:11) tells us what to do to be successful: "Put on the whole armor of God, that you may be able to stand against the wiles of the devil."

Let's look at each piece of our God-given armor.

Belt of Truth

> Stand firm then, with the belt of truth buckled around your waist. (Ephesians 6:14)

This belt of truth is the first piece of armor, and it's the most essential, because it holds everything together. How? Without the understanding and knowledge of who God is, it's impossible to survive.

What is the truth? Jesus answered, "I am the way and the truth and the life. No one comes to the Father except through me" (John 14:6). We must make sure that we remain in the truth of who Christ is. Who is Christ? He is God in the flesh, carrying eternal life through the blood that He shed for us. We must be operating under the power of that blood continually, not relying on anything else, including, but not limited to, religions, denominations, preachers, counselors, possessions, or even other relationships. The truth is in the blood of the Lamb! Truth protects us from deceit. Matthew 24:4 says, "Watch out that no one deceives you."

Breastplate of Righteousness

> With the breastplate of righteousness in place. (Ephesians 6:14)

When we hear the word "righteousness," we often think of perfection, purity, super holiness, and a floating-on-a-cloud scenario; however, true righteousness simply means being right with God. It doesn't mean that being right with God doesn't include one or more of the above, but it's not anything we can do on our own. Instead, it's having the right relationship with our Father, and the only way we can have that is through His Son, Jesus, which takes us back to our first piece of armor. Therefore, we must make sure that this breastplate of being right with God covers our most vital "organs," because the devil knows he can permanently disable us if he can get to these sensitive parts. Praise God, this breastplate protects us.

Shoes: The Gospel of Peace

And with your feet fitted with the readiness that comes from the gospel of peace. (Ephesians 6:15)

What is the "gospel of peace"? Many believe this is a passive message of a baby in a manger who grew up to be a man martyred on a cross. That simply isn't the case. "Gospel" means "good news," but it's only good news for those who "believe"—and it's very bad news for those who don't.

Biblical peace isn't the same peace we encounter when war is absent or when everything is going our way. It's the assurance of knowing that we rest in God's everlasting arms through His Son. We wear this news of confidence on our feet not only because it gets us around to preach this truth, but because it's everything we stand on.

How can we even share the Gospel if we're not assured that it is God who is sending us? Romans 10:15 says, "How can anyone preach unless they are sent?" Since the Bible says we sit with Jesus at the Father's right hand, when we put on the shoes of peace, He protects our feet from the enemy.

The Lord said to my Lord: "Sit at my right hand until I put your enemies under your feet." (Matthew 22:44)

Shield of Faith

In addition to all this, take up the shield of faith, with which you
can extinguish all the flaming arrows of the evil one. (Ephesians
6:16)

Above all? Wow! This must mean it's at the top of the armor list, and
rightfully so, because "without faith, it is impossible to please God"
(Hebrews 11:6). But what is faith? It's the "things we hope for and the
evidence of things not seen" (Hebrews 11:1). In other words, it's what we
know will come to pass, such as our eternal salvation with the Father in
our heavenly home. Further, faith is the proof of things that can't appear
in the natural; they're viewed and understood only in the supernatural.
This part of our armor is essential, because we're fighting a force that isn't
visible in this natural realm. Most people around us, both friends and
family, will not even understand what we are doing. Faith is a shield that
protects us from adversity, whether our adversary is known or unknown.

Helmet of Salvation

Take the helmet of salvation… (Ephesians 6:17a)

A helmet protects the brain, our mind. Why is this helmet essential?
Because we (and only we) have the mind of Christ, and if the enemy can
get into our thoughts and belief system, he can disarm us big time—
and down we go. The devil attempts to do this through false religion,
ungodly intimate relationships, and even our emotions. That's why
Christ said we should guard our thoughts! There's no better way to protect ourselves than with the helmet of salvation.

David Heavener

Sword of the Spirit

And the sword of the Spirit, which is the word of God. And pray in the Spirit on all occasions with all kinds of prayers and requests. (Ephesians 6:17–18)

Now we come to the only part of the armor that is a weapon of offense: the sword. The sword is the Word of God, the Scripture, His instructions to us. This is our only weapon that can take out the enemy, because it contains God's perfect plan for us; it is His instructions on fighting this battle. In fact, we might call it "the battle plan."

God's Word is the lethal weapon against the enemy.

For the word of God is alive and active. Sharper than any double-edged sword, it penetrates even to dividing soul and spirit, joints and marrow; it judges the thoughts and attitudes of the heart. (Hebrews 4:12)

Wow! That's power!

A well-trained street fighter knows how to defend himself from deadly blows. He waits until the perfect opportunity to deliver the all-powerful punch that takes out the opponent. In the same way, we, as God's warriors in heaven's army, must use the same tactics, knowing it's just as essential to *defend* ourselves against the enemy as it is to fight on the offense. In battle, we must understand that a warrior uses a sword to block the opponent's assault until the opportunity arises to deliver that fatal blow. The Sword of the Spirit—the Word of God—is both an offensive and defensive weapon.

Now that's what I call power's best friend: protection.

Power Thieves

The thief comes only to steal and kill and destroy; I have come that they may have life, and have it to the full.
JOHN 10:10, NKJV

From the moment we are conceived, Satan focuses on our destruction. He plans to steal our power and take away our strength. Let's take a look at some of the tactics that Satan uses to thwart God's plan.

Education

From the time we're in kindergarten in the public school system, a rigid academic regime tells us that the only way to be happy in life is to graduate from high school and college. The world has conjured up the curriculum and gives strict guidelines necessary for success—according to its definition. This educational system is designed to mind-control students. Most of the curriculum in postmodern academia is completely anti-Christian. It hinges on ideas such as moral relativism, political correctness, and even religious dogma—but one that is anything but biblical. Many young people are hoodwinked into going into debt and are brainwashed with a luciferian agenda—to acquire a piece of paper called a diploma. As so many students discover, the promise that a degree will guarantee a good job is false. In other words, it's a carefully constructed lie, and in the desperate pursuit of a diploma, God's intent for one's life can get easily waylaid or smothered by the world's agenda.

Spirit of Religion

Many churches are designed to take away one's power. The moment we enter these churches, we're given a "bulletin"—a leaflet presenting the order of service telling us what will happen and when, and the bullet points of the sermon. With this, we become merely members of the audience. The preacher is the star of the show. We're programmed to believe we're not qualified to know or understand God's Word without the pastor's help. All that's required of us is to pay attention to the pastor's speech and fill in the blanks on the handout. We become convinced that we must listen to what the preacher has to say and to lean on every word as if it's the Gospel in the present. The church congregation follows the tradition of the denomination (or of that particular church). This can cause people to lose their power to think as individuals, or—even worse—it can compel them to become victims of a corrupt religious system. This promotes Satan's system—a religious web that slowly entangles its victims through false teachings and the doctrine of secular humanism. Moreover, those in church leadership rarely talk directly about spiritual power and, at best, many give a "relevant" sermon about relationships, finances, or careers—but they sweep our true power under the rug.

Authority Is Good (If It's *Good*)

Scripture does say we should have order in the church and people appointed to leadership positions. However, many in authority don't know how the early church operated. They only understand the practices of their denomination or tradition. This is often why religious abuse goes on in the church today: Most members feel they're there to observe rather than participate in the services.

Why is this?

It's because of the satanic spirits operating among God's children. These demonic entities manifest in the realm of money, power, and hatred for the truth.

Let's break this down and take a closer look.

Scripture tells us the nature and goal of Satan and his henchmen. In fact, 1 Peter 5:8 warns:

Be alert and of sober mind. Your enemy, the devil, prowls around like a roaring lion looking for someone to devour.

Satan doesn't rest. He doesn't stop seeking to destroy what God has established. Jesus spoke further on the nature of Satan when He addressed the Pharisees in John 8:44:

You belong to your father, the devil, and you want to carry out your father's desires. He was a murderer from the beginning, not holding to the truth, for there is no truth in him. When he lies, he speaks his native language, for he is a liar and the father of lies.

Here, Jesus told us that Satan is a killer and a liar. His native language is that of lies, and he is trying to destroy the church by mixing his lies with God's truth in order to deceive as many people as possible. Satan waters down the Gospel, diluting its power and keeping us from reaching our full-power potential. Many pastors and church leaders have been compromised and follow their father, the devil, rather than God the Father. We don't need a magnifying glass to see the obvious.

Satan has infiltrated the church. The sin that was once corrected is now excused.

Tolerance: The "New" Love

Political correctness is another of Satan's divisive tools that keeps Christians from speaking out and calling sin what it is. The Lord commands us to love everyone, but He also instructs us to rebuke sin. Would a loving person casually allow someone else to continue down a path to eternal damnation to avoid hurting his or her feelings? To allow someone to continue living in sin without reproach is not love. God is love, and He rebukes those He loves. We are called to love; therefore, we are called to rebuke. One of the most frequently misused Scripture verses is Matthew 7:1, "Judge not, that ye be not judged" (NKJV). Whether they're engaging in adultery, greediness, or homosexuality, people living in sin often use this verse as a get-out-of-jail-free card. Many flippantly say, "Only *God* can judge me," without any awareness of the severity of His judgment. It is better to be judged by a person solely for the sake of deliverance from God's wrath. We fall for the enemy's tactic when we hear and accept only half-truths from Scripture.

I've noticed a pattern in many churches today wherein the preachers deliver only positive, safe, cookie-cutter messages. Many times, they back their sermon with Scripture that's taken out of context. Even pastors who seem to nail certain subjects often pervert their conclusions to avoid offending anyone—but who are they afraid of offending?

In many congregations, a remnant of God's people is hungry for the Gospel. However, they're overshadowed by the rest of the congregation (who may not be saved.) Are the unsaved the ones writing the fat checks? Preachers caught in the system of "feeding the flock and keeping the peace" are victims of Satan's dirty plan to destroy souls.

Can Grand Theft Occur in the Church?

Unfortunately, the church is where Satan is most active. If God's people would only use their power, then Satan couldn't have such free rein. Sure, there would be a confrontation, but if so, congratulations! Doing such a thing puts one in good company! Our Lord always confronted the religious sector with the truth. Why should we be any different? Jesus said in John 14:12, "They will do even greater things than these," and in Matthew 10:22, "You will be hated by everyone because of me." We shouldn't worry so much about hurting people's feelings; we should be more concerned about their eternal salvation.

So, how can we take charge of an apostate church? Matthew 18:15 explains the godly method:

> If your brother or sister sins, go and point out their fault, just between the two of you. If they listen to you, you have won them over.

So first, to address the issues in an apostate church, we should go to the primary source—the pastor. There's no need to talk to anyone else, even if it's a deacon or an elder. They may interpret our efforts as gossip. It's helpful to write down our concerns and, during the conversation, to be very gentle but firm. If the pastor opens up to engage in an honest dialogue, we only need to wait patiently on the seed to see if something grows. If he seems to dodge the issue or deny the problem, it's time to go to the next step, which is outlined in Matthew 18:16–17:

> But if they will not listen, take one or two others along, so that "every matter may be established by the testimony of two or three witnesses." If they still refuse to listen, tell it to the church; and if they refuse to listen even to the church, treat them as you would a pagan or a tax collector.

This can be difficult; however, if we believe God wants His children to stand on truth, then we must believe He will back us up as we go into this spiritual warfare at the next level. It's crucial to be proactive and ensure that the truth is being taught. We must break the pattern of being only an audience member during worship services. We're not called to be mere spectators; we're called to be active participants.

The church system is in sad shape. Unless we, as God's elect, step up and use our power, there will be weeping and gnashing of teeth, according to Luke 13:28. The above steps apply to conflicts with the pastor and church leaders and to issues between fellow believers. Again, disagreement between two true believers—especially when it involves a spiritual matter—has no place in a worldly courtroom judged by worldly authorities. There is a time when the true believer must simply walk away, though I don't believe it happens very often when we seek the Holy Spirit for God's direction in all matters.

Our job is to speak the truth and spread the saving, life-changing message of the Gospel of Jesus Christ. If we let Satan rob us of the power, we lose the ability to fulfill the Great Commission Jesus gave us. Remember, Satan is a liar, but Jesus is truth. Lies create bondage while truth sets us free. In the words of our precious Savior, we look at the power thief and state clearly, "Get thee behind me, Satan" (Matthew 16:23 KJV). These words stop the power thief dead in his tracks.

9

The Power of Positive Thinking Is a Lie

Trust in the Lord with all thine heart;
and lean not unto thine own understanding.
In all thy ways acknowledge him, and he shall direct thy paths.

PROVERBS 3:5–6, KJV

Many years ago, I came across a video series called *The Secret*. As I watched, God showed me the enemy's tactics and agenda: to deceive people into being their own god. The thought process espoused in *The Secret* leads readers to believe they can merely think into existence a better job, more money, a great life mate, and so forth. In essence, the message telegraphed in this video series is that one can "positively think" one's future into reality. Unfortunately, this New Age, positive thinking has seeped into the modern-day church. Seeker-friendly churches want to motivate their captive audience with secular humanism and mind control, meanwhile filling their own pockets rather than winning souls.

The positive-thinking movement is blessing many people here on earth with what seems to be their best life; however, it's a counterfeit belief system that can lead to hell. It is growing like a cancer across the Western world and even into third-world countries. This "gospel," dubbed the "prosperity gospel" or the "health-and-wealth gospel" is a "name-it-and-claim-it" creed that continues to lure thousands of people into a web of deceit. The idea is that there is power in thinking positively, and whatever we can imagine, we can make happen. This leads to health, wealth, and personal power, so the story goes. Preachers and teachers of this doctrine view God as a genie who is willing to grant anything we want. The focus becomes not what we can do for our Creator and Lord, but what He can do for us—what "wishes" can He grant?

Of course I'm not saying that God doesn't want to bless His people. He states that He is willing for us to prosper, as we read in 3 John 1:2, among other passages:

> Beloved, I wish above all things that thou mayest prosper and be in health, even as thy soul prospereth. (KJV)

The danger, however, is thinking that if we're not prospering (especially according to a worldly perspective), we must have sin in our life. That could be true; however, this thinking can lead many to believe that God doesn't love them because they face trials and aren't abounding in worldly riches. (This completely ignores the number of saints who have been persecuted and martyred for the sake of the Gospel.)

The Apostle Peter told us not to think it strange to be dealing with hard times:

> Dear friends, do not be surprised at the fiery ordeal that has come on you to test you, as though something strange were happening to you. But rejoice inasmuch as you participate in the sufferings of Christ, so that you may be overjoyed when his glory is revealed. If you are insulted because of the name of Christ, you are blessed, for the Spirit of glory and God rests on you. (1 Peter 4:12–14)

Many of us will face tough times and trials, and God warns us not to be shocked when that happens. If anything, the Christian life promises suffering. Sharing in Christ's sufferings indicates that we're doing something right.

The prosperity gospel is a clever ploy of Satan to convince those dealing with bad times that something is wrong with them and that God the Father doesn't love them because He is refusing to give them what they want. Satan used this tactic in the Garden of Eden when he tempted Eve to eat the forbidden fruit. Satan asked Eve why a loving God wouldn't want her to have the fruit. God's Word tells us in Matthew 6:33:

> But seek first his kingdom and his righteousness, and all these things will be given to you as well.

God knows and sees what we don't. We know His character is that of a loving Father.

As Jesus said in Luke 11:11–13:

> Which of you fathers, if your son asks for a fish, will give him a snake instead? Or if he asks for an egg, will give him a scorpion? If you then, though you are evil, know how to give good gifts to your children, how much more will your Father in heaven give the Holy Spirit to those who ask him!

There is power in thinking, but the power isn't in "positive" thinking. The true power is in godly thinking. Paul says in 1 Corinthians 2:16 that we have the "mind of the Lord" if we are born again. It's not the fact *that* we think, it's *what* we think. Positive thinking is only a danger when directed toward ourselves and not God, and it's only a sin when we focus on our power and not God's.

Make Sure the Security Guard Is on Duty

When the guard sleeps, criminals break in and steal our spiritual discernment, so it is a top priority to guard our thoughts, as Romans 12:2 reminds us:

> Do not conform to the pattern of this world, but be transformed by the renewing of your mind. Then you will be able to test and approve what God's will is—his good, pleasing and perfect will.

How can children of God guard their thoughts? Here are three ways:

1. **Pray.** Praying is talking directly with God. We often ask Him for better health, more money, safety, wisdom, and whatever else we need at the time. However, how often have we specifically asked the Father for power or for an understanding of how to use the power He has already given us? We don't usually do that, because it might sound too egotistical. But there is incredible power in a prayer along the lines of the following: "Lord, please help me understand and use the authority and power your Son Jesus transferred to me—power so that I can continue the work you have commissioned me to do, power that protects me, and power that glorifies you. Amen."

2. **Read Scripture.** There are two ways to read Scripture: with our mind or with God's. Since we have the mind of Christ, we can ask the Holy Spirit to increase our Christ-mind with understanding and do what Scripture intends. We read in 2 Timothy 3:16–17 that "all Scripture is God-breathed and is useful for teaching, rebuking, correcting and training in righteousness, so that the servant of God may be thoroughly equipped for every good work." Now that's true power!

3. **Test the spirits.** I can't overemphasize the importance of being aware of our surroundings and our friends. As Christians, we live in the spiritual realm, yet we continue placing emphasis on physical matters. This is one way the enemy can attack us. Many believers pray, read Scripture, and try to live as they believe God would have them live, yet their lives are messy. A closer look may reveal that they have made poor choices concerning their relationships and/or their environment. We need to heed the words in 1 John 4:1–3, which says:

Dear friends, do not believe every spirit, but test the spirits to see whether they are from God, because many false prophets have gone out into the world. This is how you can recognize the Spirit of God: Every spirit that acknowledges that Jesus Christ has come in the flesh is from God, but every spirit that does not acknowledge Jesus is not from God. This is the spirit of the antichrist, which you have heard is coming and even now is already in the world.

The evil one is here. Scripture says he has come out from among us. Christians may need to get out of toxic relationships and situations in which they're being used or even abused. Jesus says, "If anyone will not welcome you or listen to your words, leave that home or town and shake the dust off your feet" (Matthew 10:14). As God's elect, we must constantly be on high alert.

Instead of believing in the power of positive thinking, we can be positive about His ability to give us the correct thinking and trust entirely that God will take care of us. That's where the true power is.

"For my thoughts are not your thoughts, neither are your ways my ways," declares the Lord. "As the heavens are higher than the earth, so are my ways higher than your ways and my thoughts than your thoughts." (Isaiah 55:8–9)

The Power of Birthright

What good is it for someone to gain the whole world,
yet forfeit their soul?
MARK 8:36

According to Scripture, in Jewish culture, the oldest son receives a birthright; he is favored and receives the inheritance—the power.

Once when Jacob was cooking some stew, Esau came in from the open country, famished. He said to Jacob, "Quick, let me have some of that red stew. I'm famished." Jacob replied, "First sell me your birthright." "Look, I am about to die," Esau said. "What good is the birthright to me?" But Jacob said, "Swear to me first." So he swore an oath to him, selling his birthright to Jacob. Then Jacob gave Esau some bread and some lentil stew. He ate and drank, and then got up and left. So Esau despised his birthright. (Genesis 25:29–34)

When Christ left the earth as a man, He gave us an inheritance, and part of that inheritance was authority over the evil one and the power to crush serpents.

I have given you authority to trample on snakes and scorpions and to overcome all the power of the enemy; nothing will harm you. (Luke 10:19)

Like Esau, many have traded their inheritance—their power—for immediate pleasure and self-fulfilling desires, like the bowl of soup.

What Is Our Bowl of Soup?

What are we giving up our position and power for? Is it for popularity? Money? Worldly power? Lust? We trade against our birthright daily. However, unlike Esau, we can change that right now. We can stop selling out and start loving God and doing what pleases Him more than what pleases us and others. Have you been an Esau for too long? Be a Jacob by valuing your power, and stop being an Esau, who hated his.

The process of employing God's power, illustrated below, is similar to guarding our thoughts discussed in the previous chapter. Failure to guard our thoughts will result in an inability to use God's power properly; Esau did not guard his thoughts. He was carnally minded. He relinquished his position and the rights attached to it, and he fulfilled his immediate fleshly desires. With a disciplined and guarded mind and a firm grip on God's power, here's how to employ God's power:

1. Read Scripture. Jesus said in Matthew 22:29, "You are in error because you do not know the Scriptures or the power of God." He wasn't saying they didn't have Scripture in their head. I'm sure many had it memorized and quoted it often. He was saying they didn't *understand* it. When we dwell in the Spirit, we have access to the power and knowledge of the Spirit. First John 2:27 says:

As for you, the anointing you received from him remains in you, and you do not need anyone to teach you. But as his anointing teaches you about all things and as that anointing is real, not counterfeit—just as it has taught you, remain in him.

How do we stay in Him? Through communicating and being in a relationship. Scripture is God speaking to us; we also communicate with Him through prayer.

2. Pray. We don't need to pray for power. As God's children, we already have it. There is power in prayer, however. Without dwelling in the Spirit, it is impossible to ultimately come to God with an understanding of our position. For example: When my children approach me to ask for something, they know my character, they know their relationship with me, and they understand their position in our family as my true children and I as their father. Typically, I'm delighted to grant their request (if it's within my capability). If neighbors approach me with requests, however, it's different. They don't know me. Therefore, they don't know how to ask me for something; it's awkward. It's the same with God and His children. We have this promise given to us in 1 John 5:14:

This is the confidence we have in approaching God: that if we ask anything according to his will, he hears us.

3. Dwell in the Spirit, our source of power. This is one reason God's children stray off the beaten path of their purpose. Like a boat in the ocean with a motor to drive and guide it, we have a motor, and it's called power. When we don't use our power, we're like a boat drifting with the current. It usually takes us to a huge waterfall, and there we are, drifting to our doom, trying to paddle away from destruction, when all we need to do is *turn on the motor*. Turn on the *power*. We don't need to "name it and claim it"; the name is the Holy Spirit. There is no claiming to be done, because if we're true believers, then we have the power already: the Holy Spirit is our source of power.

Don't you know that you yourselves are God's temple and that God's Spirit dwells in your midst? (1 Corinthians 3:16)

It's time for us to stop compromising, take back our rightful inheritance, and start living like God's true children. Our heritage is waiting for us to reclaim it, its eternal value is unmatched, and no force can separate us from it; it's up to us to take back what's rightfully ours—our spiritual birthright. We are *His* reflection. Each time we look in the mirror, instead of seeing a mere mortal, we are gazing upon God's power—our birthright.

That's the power of our inheritance.

The Power of Knowing

Have you ever heard people say, "I know that I know," and they're so sure of something that they just *know*? This kind of knowing isn't a matter of understanding; rather, it's a state of believing—a condition of the heart and mind wherein there is no room for doubt, no matter the circumstances or even what seem to be hard-core facts. When people are in a state of "knowing," they're usually immovable, untouchable, and unstoppable. Why? This "knowing" originates from the Spirit and is so embedded in the belief system that it's impossible to tamper with its power. There are three primary stages before we reach the final state of knowing:

Stage 1: Seeing God and knowing He exists, but not being connected with Him.
Stage 2: Being connected with God, but still living as though we are
separate from Him.
Stage 3: Being connected with God to the extent that we can't tell
the difference between ourselves and our Heavenly Father.

These stages of knowing depict most of mankind and how we are (or aren't) connected spiritually to God. The first stage is where most are. They know there is a god they call a "higher power," a "master of the universe," or "the man upstairs," but they have no real connection with this god, only believing that he (or she) rules somewhere "up there."

The second stage is where, sadly, most churchgoers live. They connect with God at some level, always trying to do something to get closer to their interpretation of "godliness." They go to church every week, rock out to the latest Christian worship songs, or become involved in religious sensationalism such as false "signs and wonders." There is an appearance of godliness, but no authentic relationship with God.

Then there is the third stage, where every child of God should strive to be, especially to do God's work; otherwise, we become like the seed cast on the ground that fails to take root. Unless we are in this phase, we are useless. This is when we're so ingrained in our belief about God and His truth for us that we can't tell the difference between ourselves and God. Let me clarify: I'm not saying that we think we *are* God, but rather that we are *inseparable from* Him.

Babies don't know they are separate beings as they gaze upon their mother, thinking they are one. This is how we must be with God—enjoying oneness with Him, having complete unity with our Creator, so much so that others can't tell where our humanity ends and our spiritual nature begins. This separates true spirituality from religiosity. Jesus desired that we be *one* with Him and the Father, as *He* and the Father are one. Christ also asked the Father that we all can be one; all of God's chosen can come together as one so the world can know that God is real, and sent His Son.

Is there a solution? The question is, how do we achieve this third phase of *knowing* God? How can we get to the point that we're so united with Him that we "walk as one?" The answer is simple: By loving Him. "Love Him? Of course, I love Him." This is the response from most people who have been spiritually brainwashed into thinking love is a feeling, emotion, and a continuous act of religiosity. To know what real love is, we must turn to God's Word. Yes, the key to loving in the third stage of knowing God is not only reading His Word, but living in it and applying it to our lives. Through prayer and the guidance of the Holy Spirit, God supernaturally reveals Himself to us.

Most believers use 1 Corinthians 13:4–7 as their "love thermometer":

Love is patient, love is kind. It does not envy, it does not boast, it is not proud. It does not dishonor others, it is not self-seeking, it is not easily angered, it keeps no record of wrongs. Love does not delight in evil but rejoices with the truth. It always protects, always trusts, always hopes, always perseveres.

While this passage does deal with the fruit of God's love, it is not His love (or our love for Him), but rather the result of genuinely loving Him. This has led many people down a false path of security, believing that if they do the things mentioned in 1 Corinthians chapter 13, they have it made, and are really living out God's definition of true love. However, that's not the case. First John 5:3 defines how to love God:

In fact, this is love for God: to keep his commands. And his commands are not burdensome.

Yes, we love God by *keeping His commandments*. They aren't meant to be a burden. The "pulpit wolves" have manipulated the term "commandments" by teaching that when Jesus came, He abolished God's laws and teachings of the prophets. Christ, however, detailed the truth: He did not come to *abolish* the Law, but to *fulfill* it.

Do not think that I have come to abolish the Law or the Prophets; I have not come to abolish them but to fulfill them. For truly I tell you until heaven and earth disappear, not the smallest letter, not the least stroke of a pen, will by any means disappear from the Law until everything is accomplished. (Matthew 5:17–18)

God's Word today holds true to His Old Testament laws and the prophets' words. No part of His Word should be omitted. So, what is the Law, and what were the prophets proclaiming? The answer could be a chapter in itself, but the bottom line is *there is no such thing as an Old Testament and a New Testament.* This division is a man-made deception to get people believing that there are two truths and two separate messages from God to His people. *There is only one Bible, one truth, and one message to God's people.* It's the Word of God, and it's not two separate entities.

Here are the steps we can take to study and understand God's commandments:

1. We can have a real meeting with God to ask Him to clean our religious house of anything and everything in our hearts, minds, and belief systems that is counterfeit; we can ask Him to take it away and give us a true hunger for His Word and truth.
2. We can read and research the Scriptures, starting with Genesis, while also researching the Jewish culture and how it guides us into a true relationship with Jesus.
3. As God leads, we can share this newfound truth with others, especially the preachers.

Why do I emphasize sharing our understanding with the preachers? Let's look at what Christ goes on to say in Matthew 5:19–20:

Therefore anyone who sets aside one of the least of these commands and teaches others accordingly will be called least in the kingdom of heaven, but whoever practices and teaches these commands will be called great in the kingdom of heaven. For I tell you that unless your righteousness surpasses that of the Pharisees and the teachers of the law, you will certainly not enter the kingdom of heaven.

The Pharisees were the religious leaders of the time and were regarded as being the most righteous. They knew the Word of God better than anyone; however, they were farther away from God because they didn't understand His Word and character. The same is true of today's pastors who cherry-pick ideas and statements from the Bible, misconstrue those issues to adapt to their flock's "needs," water down any truth in what they've learned, and lead people astray. We must be more righteous than the deceptive "religious" people. That is possible only if we know right from wrong through the lens of God's Word.

That's the power in knowing.

12

The Power of Gone

He could not do any miracles there, except lay his
hands on a few sick people and heal them.

MARK 6:5

Many interpretations of this verse don't sit well with me. I've heard some preachers suggest that Christ *could not* use His power rather than that He *chose* not to use it. Looking at God's character tells us that human weakness has never dictated the measure of God's power. On the contrary, when we are weak, God commands us to stand on His power. Second Corinthians 12:10 says:

> I delight in weaknesses, in insults, in hardships, in persecutions, in difficulties. For when I am weak, then I am strong.

When Jesus went to Nazareth, the place His family had considered home once they returned from Egypt, the flood of miracles that usually accompanied His arrival in an area was missing due to the people's unbelief. This incident reinforces what Jesus said in Matthew 13:57:

> And they took offense at him. But Jesus said to them, "A prophet is not without honor except in his own town and in his own home."

Because of their lack of faith, Christ healed only a few, though it wasn't as much due to their unbelief as it was because of Christ's desire for respect and honor. When God is dishonored, He leaves; He is gone. That might sound pretty drastic, but what I mean is that God's power has "left the building," so to speak. Of course, He has patience and love for us, and He demonstrates it every time we breathe, but the Father never allows anyone to disrespect Him.

For example: Imagine a man sitting in a park. He begins cursing God at the top of his lungs. He screams curses, requests God's blessing, then follows with more expletives. Not only is God gone, but I'd feel nervous standing next to this individual for fear of a "stray" bolt of lightning.

Consider another example: Imagine a wife working in her kitchen, making dinner while her husband is at work. When a song comes on the radio, she remembers a special dinner she and her husband had a few years ago. That brings a smile to her face. Happily, she hums a little song as she sets the table, arranges a few flowers, and muses over setting out candles. Absence makes the heart grow fonder. Her husband then comes home from work, slams the door, and insults and curses her. He then asks what's for dinner. He'd be fortunate not to have his dinner thrown at him. His wife would probably get the car keys and leave, if not forever, for a while. All those good feelings would be gone.

But wait! What about grace? You know, the things the preacher says about God's unending love and tolerance? Well, first of all, Scripture never mentions God's limitless patience for sin, and maybe your pastor never taught the "there will be weeping and gnashing of teeth" Scripture in Luke 13:28. As for grace, let's look at 2 Corinthians 12:9:

But he said to me, "My grace is sufficient for you, for my power is made perfect in weakness." Therefore I will boast all the more gladly about my weaknesses, so that Christ's power may rest on me.

Now, does that "grace" sound like God's power is only as good as our level of belief? No. Therefore, the theory that God's power is measured or manipulated by our unbelief is absurd. On the contrary, our weakness manifests God's power in us. For example, in Mark 6:7–10, our Lord sent His disciples to do exactly what He was doing—exercising power over unclean spirits. He gave them the details:

> Calling the Twelve to him, he began to send them out two by two and gave them authority over impure spirits. These were his instructions: "Take nothing for the journey except a staff—no bread, no bag, no money in your belts. Wear sandals but not an extra shirt. Whenever you enter a house, stay there until you leave that town."

In the next verse, He prepared them to encounter what He experienced: unbelief and rejection.

> And if any place will not welcome you or listen to you, leave that place and shake the dust off your feet as a testimony against them. Verily I say unto you, it shall be more tolerable for Sodom and Gomorrah in the day of judgment, than for that city. (Mark 6:11)

Here's a perfect example of the power of "gone." Christ tells us to get out of certain situations. But we, with our misunderstanding of Scripture, feel it is "Christ-like" to hang around people who reject the truth. So, there we stand, getting abused emotionally, mentally, verbally, and spiritually while we try to preach the Gospel, and we think this is what God wants. Nope. God shows us that we have the power to walk away, to be gone. God did not design us to be doormats.

Gather Our Pearls and Go Home

Many face abuse from family, friends, and the church when they use God's power. But, rather than leaving as Christ commands, they stay. Their excuse is, "I need to stay and love them, be compassionate, and tolerate the abuse because that's the Christ-like thing to do. That's what Jesus would do."

The truth is, Jesus never stayed in His hometown very long. He left. Furthermore, He *never* instructed His disciples to remain in any town and suffer abuse; instead, He told them to do the opposite: Shake the dust off their feet. Be gone. (Mark 6:11)

Shaking off dust was a gesture symbolizing that the disciples were moving on; they had done all they could. People who rejected the disciples' message were denying the Lord, and they weren't worthy to cling to the feet of those bringing the good news.

> Do not give dogs what is sacred; do not throw your pearls to pigs. If you do, they may trample them under their feet, and turn and tear you to pieces. (Matthew 7:6)

We are royalty; therefore, we should act like children of the King. As Christians, we're not doormats for religious spirits to use for housekeeping, to lay down heavy burdens of erroneous doctrine each week.

Be gone. Why? Because there is another town, church, or Bible study up the road waiting for the King's children to bring God's power and truth. We must not waste our time and energy on the dead.

> Jesus said to him, "Let the dead bury their own dead, but you go and proclaim the kingdom of God." (Luke 9:60)

That's the power of *gone*.

13

The Power of Recharging

I'll never forget the camping trip when I awoke in my tent in the middle of the night, needing to go out to find a bathroom. It was pitch dark. I grabbed my flashlight and turned it on, only to discover the battery was dead. How could that be? I had never even used the flashlight except maybe once the year before. Then my wife said to me, "David, batteries go bad when they aren't used." Wow! What a perfect example of our "spiritual battery." How many Christians seldom use their spiritual battery—or never use it at all? The result is a dead faith with no power.

The word "power" comes from the Latin word *potere*, which means "to be able." We, with God's power, are much more than able. We are supercharged! However, as I've said before, most Christians don't even know that God's power is available, so they journey through life with a dead battery.

Is a Christian with dead batteries even a Christian? I'm going to say something drastic, and it might seem unloving and perhaps even a bit hard-hearted. Christians who don't even realize they can use their power may not be held accountable. However, Christians who understand they have the power and can use it, yet decide not to, will be held responsible. Luke 12:48 says:

But the one who does not know and does things deserving punishment will be beaten with few blows. From everyone who has been given much, much will be demanded; and from the one who has been entrusted with much, much more will be asked.

A half-powered battery doesn't count. Jesus warned what would happen to those who remain lukewarm in Revelation 3:16:

So, because you are lukewarm—neither hot nor cold—I am about to spit you out of my mouth.

This "spitting out," of course, means "to vomit," and when the body vomits something out, it does so because those contents are not agreeable to the body. One reason a person vomits is to rid the body of poison. I'm sure that most will agree that the concept of Jesus deeming us poison to the His Body and expelling us from His presence is something to avoid at all costs. The solution to prevent this? Charging our batteries.

How do we recharge our spiritual battery? My wife has designated a specific drawer for batteries. When I open that drawer, I sometimes notice that some of the bad batteries have leaked acid all over the good ones. When that happens, I remove those dead batteries before they ruin the rest. We're no different from batteries. To be recharged, we need to be around Spirit-filled Christians. We can take actions to recharge our batteries by feeding our minds with Scripture, earnestly fasting, praying, and seeking guidance from the Holy Spirit. Finally, we must have fellowship with like-minded believers who understand how to use their God-given power.

If you're in a powerless church, get out. If you cannot find a church that's power-filled, start a Bible study. Jesus promises in Matthew 18:20, "For where two or three are gathered together in my name, there am I in the midst of them." The "I am" part is the power of God. Be specific in your personal and group Bible studies about the blood of Jesus, the miracles and healings He performed, casting out demons and transferring our Lord's power to us. "Power" is the crucial element, and when a child of God dives into the study of it, asking the Holy Spirit to guide and reveal, marvelous things can happen. Nothing is impossible with God. Ask God to send others into your Bible study who are hungry for truth.

Third John 1:4 says:

> I have no greater joy than to hear that my children are walking in the truth.

Ask God how you can use your God-given power. Reach out to people who are sick or need encouragement and pray over them. Watch God's power kick in. See what God will do through you!

> And whatever you do, whether in word or deed, do it all in the name of the Lord Jesus, giving thanks to God the Father through him. (Colossians 3:17)

When you see someone with a need, ask if they need prayer, then pray in the power of the Holy Spirit. The more we practice using our God-given power, the more supercharged our spiritual battery will be. We heed the warning in Romans 13:2:

> Whoever rebels against the authority is rebelling against what God has instituted, and those who do so will bring judgment on themselves.

That's the power of recharging.

Power's True Source

Yet for us there is but one God, the Father,
from whom all things came and for whom we live;
and there is but one Lord, Jesus Christ, through whom all
things came and through whom we live.

1 CORINTHIANS 8:6

I t's essential to understand the power of God within us and to stay true to the *source* of power. How do we do that? Laws of electricity dictate that it must always be respected and handled with the utmost caution. One wrong move can endanger not only the electrician, but others as well.

DANGER! High Voltage

Power is dangerous when not used properly. Each year, thousands of electrical work-related injuries and deaths occur. What's one of the leading causes of death on the job? Electrocution. That happens when there is a *misuse* of electrical power, and the same goes for spiritual power. One of the most hazardous abuses of God's power is misunderstanding its origin. The source is God, through His Son, delivered by the

Holy Spirit. There is no other way, period. In Mark's account of Jesus manifesting Himself in a way no one had ever witnessed, we see how vulnerable human nature is to sensationalism, creating an error in our reasoning:

> After six days Jesus took Peter, James, and John with him and led them up a high mountain, where they were all alone. There he was transfigured before them. His clothes became dazzling white, whiter than anyone in the world could bleach them. And there appeared before them Elijah and Moses, who were talking with Jesus. Peter said to Jesus, "Rabbi, it is good for us to be here. Let us put up three shelters—one for you, one for Moses and one for Elijah." (He did not know what to say, they were so frightened.) (Mark 9:2–6)

Nothing has changed over the past two thousand years. We still tend to worship things connected to God's power or counterfeits of it. God was clearly showing His true power to mortals through this transfiguration, and in this case, Elijah and Moses appeared as well. Unfortunately, instead of focusing on the power of God's manifestation, Peter, James, and John were more concerned about who was with Jesus. Today, we sometimes give attention to angels, objects, or people—and sometimes we even lift the Holy Spirit into the place of God the Father. New-Age thinking has infected the Christian community with practices such as reading tarot cards, using Ouija boards, practicing yoga, and participating in astral projection, all of which counterfeit the Holy Spirit's power. These bogus powers are from hell, and if continued without repentance, will result in death.

Notice how quickly the Father tells these disciples precisely what He wants them to do:

> Then a cloud appeared and covered them, and a voice came from the cloud: "This is my Son, whom I love. Listen to him."

Suddenly, when they looked around, they no longer saw anyone with them except Jesus. (Mark 9:7–8)

The key is in the first verse of that passage: Listen to Jesus.

Don't listen to any spirit, and don't follow anyone other than our Lord. How do we know that we are on course? Scripture. The Word of God. The Holy Spirit will show us the devil and his deceptions when we "try the spirits" to see if they are from God. During these last days, it's more important than ever to follow our true power source, because the devil will come with many lying signs and wonders.

For false messiahs and false prophets will appear and perform great signs and wonders to deceive, if possible, even the elect. (Matthew 24:24)

There's a considerable downside to drawing power from anything other than its true source, and as a result, through the centuries, humanity has suffered. The most common examples of this have been recounted in Scripture as we read about God's people repeatedly turning away from Him to worship idols. Throughout ancient biblical history, the Jews, God's chosen people, abused and misused God's power and turned to other gods, creating their own religions.

Much of modern Christian teaching is a mockery, a counterfeit that creates a god to serve them—rather than a god for them to serve. Consequently, Jesus will say one day, "Depart from me, you workers of iniquity, I know you not" (Luke 13:27).

If Jesus were to walk the earth as a man today, I dare say most churches wouldn't recognize Him, much less let Him in to speak. He would probably do what He did in the Temple with the whip and harsh words, turning over tables and blocking the door, not letting anyone exit until He delivered the same point He made in Matthew 21:13, Luke 19:46, and Jeremiah 7:11: "You've turned my Father's house into a den of thieves."

The apostate religion derives its power not from the Father, but from Satan himself. Be vigilant when discerning the following trends: seeker-friendly, prosperity, self-help, spiritual narcissism, counterfeit tongues, miracles, and side-show deliverances. Sorcery, witchcraft, and divination channel false power and their adherents end in the lake of fire in eternal death.

A man or woman who is a medium or spiritist among you must be put to death. You are to stone them; their blood will be on their own heads. (Leviticus 20:27)

Jesus answered, "I am the way and the truth and the life. No one comes to the Father except through me." (John 14:6)

I believe it would be biblically correct to say, "Our *only* source of true power is from the Father through His Son, Christ."

The Power of Repentance

Those who decide to follow Christ have access to God's power, but they don't always know how to use it. When people ask for my testimony, I answer that I was saved at age seven, but I wasn't Spirit-filled until I reached my teens. I understand that you may raise an eyebrow at the implication that I was saved but didn't have the Holy Spirit. To clarify, I was saved, but I wasn't *using* the Holy Spirit. What does it mean to be Spirit-filled? Simply put, it's being engulfed in the presence and control of the third Person of God—the Holy Spirit. Jesus knew He was going away, back to the Father, so He told His disciples He would ask the Father to send them the Holy Spirit (the Comforter).

> And I will ask the Father, and he will give you another advocate
> to help you and be with you forever. (John 14:16)

In Acts 2:38, Peter states that we must meet specific criteria to be Spirit-filled:

> Peter replied, "Repent and be baptized, every one of you, in the
> name of Jesus Christ for the forgiveness of your sins. And you
> will receive the gift of the Holy Spirit."

First, Peter says we must repent—yes, this is the salvation part—then he mentions something entirely different from merely an act of speaking. Second, he says to be baptized. Is he saying baptism is necessary for realizing the full power of the Holy Spirit?

Without *true repentance*, there is no forgiveness of sin, and without forgiveness of sin, the Holy Spirit cannot dwell in us. He will not compete with sin. Most people sitting in church today haven't truly repented, and this is the apostate church Jesus spoke of. But here's the good news: We can truly repent. Our Lord cried, "Repent! The kingdom of God is at hand." Then, John baptized Him. I'm not saying that to be Spirit-filled, baptism is a mandate. We could ask, "Does baptism connect us with the Holy Spirit?"

If you can answer "yes" to the three question below, then congratulations, you're ready to repent and become a child of God:

1. Am I disgusted with the things of this world?
2. Do I believe God sent His Son Jesus to live, die, and rise again so that I can have eternal salvation and commune with Him?
3. Am I ready to give up everything in my life to follow God by reading Scripture, praying, telling others the truth about God, and doing things to further His kingdom?

John the Baptist said the following about the kingdom of God:

In those days John the Baptist came, preaching in the wilderness of Judea and saying, "Repent, for the kingdom of heaven has come near." (Matthew 3:1–2)

Yes, repent. The kingdom of God is about to be unveiled. Without a change in our hearts, we're unable to perceive what God reveals. As confirmation of this, Jesus also preached, "Repent, for the kingdom of heaven has come near" (Matthew 4:17).

When a sinner repents, the Holy Spirit takes up residence in that individual because we "are God's temple and…God's Spirit dwells in [our] midst" (1 Corinthians 3:16).

Below is an acrostic using the word REPENT to illustrate what it means to a Christian:

R – RIGHTEOUS: "God made him who had no sin to be sin for us so that in him, we might become the righteousness of God" (2 Corinthians 5:21).

E – ETERNAL: "I write these things to you who believe in the name of the Son of God so that you may know that you have eternal life" (1 John 5:13).

P – POWER: "By his power God raised the Lord from the dead, and he will raise us also" (1 Corinthians 6:14).

E – ENFORCEMENT: "If you love me, keep my commands" (John 14:15).

N – NOW: "'In the time of my favor I heard you, and in the day of salvation I helped you.' I tell you, now is the time of God's favor, now is the day of salvation" (2 Corinthians 6:2).

T – TAKEN: "Do not let your hearts be troubled. You believe in God; believe also in me. My Father's house has many rooms; if that were not so, would I have told you that I am going there to prepare a place for you? And if I go and prepare a place for you, I will come back and take you to be with me that you also may be where I am" (John 14:1–3).

Then Jesus came from Galilee to the Jordan to be baptized by John. But John tried to deter him, saying, "I need to be baptized by you, and do you come to me?" Jesus replied, "Let it be so now; it is proper for us to do this to fulfill all righteousness." Then John consented. (Matthew 3:13–15)

Baptism is the step to take after repentance. Our Lord Himself declares that baptism fulfills all righteousness, and righteousness simply means being right with God. Jesus says, "It is proper to do this," so if it's proper for Christ and fulfills being right with the Father, then I'd say that's reason enough for baptism.

One of the reasons His baptism was so important is that it *equipped* Him for ministry. Something happened after His baptism that was monumental in helping us understand how the Father sees baptism:

> As soon as Jesus was baptized, he went up out of the water. At that moment, heaven was opened, and he saw the Spirit of God descending like a dove and alighting on him. And a voice from heaven said, "This is my Son, whom I love; with him, I am well pleased." (Matthew 3:16–17)

Wow! Heaven opened, and the Spirit of the Living God came to earth and landed on the Son. This is power. True power. And God spoke in an audible voice, not only as a witness but as a presence. The power of God is the presence of God. When John baptized Jesus, the Holy Spirit had not yet descended on mankind to live in us as He does now. The dove's presence was a preview of how the Holy Spirit comes on us when we obey and act in righteousness. In the words of our Lord, "It is proper to do this." The act of being immersed in water in no way gives anyone automatic access to the Holy Spirit or power. Access comes only by obedience to Christ and His teachings on repentance and baptism. We cannot receive the Holy Spirit or His true power any other way than through Christ.

Like I mentioned earlier, there are two kinds of power. Simon the sorcerer is an example of someone who possessed and used Satan's power:

> Now for some time a man named Simon had practiced sorcery in the city and amazed all the people of Samaria. He boasted that he was someone great, and all the people, both high and low,

gave him their attention and exclaimed, "This man is rightly called the Great Power of God." They followed him because he had amazed them for a long time with his sorcery. (Acts 8:9–11)

Simon had the respect of the people, but the power was from an evil source. Can a worshiper of Satan repent and be saved?

But when they believed Philip as he proclaimed the good news of the Kingdom of God and the name of Jesus Christ, they were baptized, both men and women. Simon himself believed and was baptized. And he followed Philip everywhere, astonished by the great signs and miracles he saw. (Acts 8:12–13)

According to Scripture, a sorcerer accepts Christ and is baptized.

Attempted Hijack of God's Power

Satan always tries to either confiscate or counterfeit everything God does:

When the apostles in Jerusalem heard that Samaria had accepted the word of God, they sent Peter and John to Samaria. When they arrived, they prayed for the new believers there that they might receive the Holy Spirit, because the Holy Spirit had not yet come on any of them; they had simply been baptized in the name of the Lord Jesus. Then Peter and John placed their hands on them, and they received the Holy Spirit. When Simon saw that the Spirit was given at the laying on of the apostles' hands, he offered them money and said, "Give me also this ability so that everyone on whom I lay my hands may receive the Holy Spirit." Peter answered: "May your money perish with you, because you thought you could buy the gift of God with money. You have no part or share in this ministry, because your heart is not right before God. Repent of this wickedness and pray to the Lord in the hope that he may forgive you for having such a thought in your heart. For I see that you are full of bitterness and captive to sin." Then Simon answered, "Pray to the Lord for me so that nothing you have said may happen to me." (Acts 8:14–24)

Simon wanted the same power the apostles had, but for all the wrong reasons. He was seeking to make a name for himself rather than to fulfill God's purposes. Simon thought the way to receive the power was to pay for it. Peter was quick to rebuke this and said the power was a gift from God. Peter then told him his heart was wrong, and he needed to repent.

Wolves in Sheep's Clothing

From prosperity peddlers and name-it-and-claim-it, modern-day prophets to faith healers selling snake oil, Satan is working harder today than ever. Why now? Because the time he has left to deceive is short. Today, many "believers" follow these New Age philosophies and tactics wrapped up in a Judeo-Christian package.

Repentance is still the criteria. Whether Simon repented, then backslid, or never repented at all, the point is that it all comes down to repenting. Repentance is the only act that allows us to stand on the blood of Jesus. If you haven't truly repented, turned away from your sins, and made a real effort to follow Christ, don't even think of being baptized, as that would be nothing more than getting wet at best, and an abomination to God at worst. Perhaps you were baptized as a baby, or you were baptized but never really repented. The good news is that you can truly repent and be baptized, but this time for God, under the precious blood of Christ.

That, my friend, is how to receive true power.

16

The Power of Real Amazing Grace

Imagine you committed a crime. You've been tried, found guilty, and sentenced to death, and now you stand before a firing squad. There is one person who signals the squad to fire. Instead of giving the signal to shoot, however, that person says, "Disengage your weapons. Lower your rifles." Wow! You have barely escaped death. You don't deserve to be pardoned, but you are. Now, take this situation and multiply it by eternity—that's when you see a glimpse of God's grace and, perhaps, the best word to describe this kind of grace: *mercy*. When people show mercy, it's not because they reconsider the severity of the crime. It's because they remove the penalty of the punishment.

The God of Grace

Much of the modern church has created a hyper-grace movement wherein grace is God, instead of God being grace. Preachers craft sermons to make churchgoers feel deserving. In contrast, the truth is that the moment we feel deserving is the moment we risk losing our position of grace. Attention prosperity preacher: Put that in your $100 million jet and smoke it! God's grace is *not* what we stand on. It's what we *bow* to. When we think of God's grace, perhaps what comes to mind is leniency, kindheartedness, or gentleness. While these certainly are some of the Father's characteristics, they're not the core of His grace.

The hyper-grace movement teaches, "Do what you want when you want. God is always there waiting for you to fall so He can pick you up." It is almost as if God is an enabler, not much different from a drug dealer providing dope and then waiting for addicts to overdose so He can bring them back to life. Wow! What a hero. Wait—did I say "hero"? Could this explain why religion preaches a false grace? Is it so that the religious system can be the hero when we fall, rescuing the flock while always maintaining control? Is it about mind, money, and soul control? This sounds like a familiar religious system that existed when Christ walked the earth.

> Woe to you, teachers of the law and Pharisees, you hypocrites.
> You travel over land and sea to win a single convert, and when
> you have succeeded, you make them twice as much a child of
> hell as you are. (Matthew 23:15)

From Amazing Grace to Amazing Disgrace

I don't hear many churches singing "Amazing Grace" in its original form anymore; most sing the song with the words changed. Compare the original and modern lyrics to see what critical point is intentionally left out:

Original version: "Amazing grace! How sweet the sound / That saved a wretch like me."

Updated ("safe") version: "Amazing grace! How sweet the sound / That saved and set me free."

That's it! One crucial word: "wretch."

The manipulation of the meaning of this particular song is perhaps the best example we have of how Satan perverts the true gospel of grace. While the words of the revised version are still true, they overshadow the intent of the original message. What message? Grace saves. But it saves only those willing to admit they are broken, distraught, and wretched.

> For by grace, you have been saved through faith; and that not of yourselves, it is the gift of God. (Ephesians 2:8)

The only way to receive salvation is to realize that there is grace, and through this realization, we discover the real meaning of grace—the true amazing grace.

"My chains are gone / I've been set free." These words are also found in an updated version of the hymn. But I have a problem with this version as well. I believe it omits the necessary condition of the heart—humility.

> But He gives more grace. Therefore it says, "God opposes the proud, but gives grace to the humble." (James 4:6)

There is no "being set free"—or amazing grace—unless we first have the heart's condition called humility. We cannot obtain grace if we don't recognize our need for it and what it saves us from. Today's apostate church has twisted Scripture to further their agenda of feel-good, prosperous, "best life now" on earth. They do it by leaving out the true meaning of humility and replacing it with a false gospel. As of the writing of this book, many churches are still closed due to the COVID-19 pandemic shutdown. Make no mistake, though, the wolves in sheep's clothing still operate through the Internet to spread a gospel of false grace.

The Power of True Grace

> However, I consider my life worth nothing to me; my only aim is to finish the race and complete the task the Lord Jesus has given me—the task of testifying to the good news of God's grace. (Acts 20:24)

Wow! Grace is the fuel in our spiritual tank that gets us over the finish line to win the race and testify what God has done for us. Yes, God has "saved a wretch like me. / I once was lost, but now I'm found / was blind, but now I see."

Thank You for Loving Me to Death

What was it that Christ did for us? He *died* for us, whereby unfolding true grace so that we may tell others about this amazing grace. Remember that person I mentioned earlier—the one in charge of the firing squad who had to execute a punishment for your crime? He put His Son in *your* place. He took the burden of your crime upon His Beloved Only Son. As believers, that truth humbles us; it makes us want to serve the one who gave us mercy. It makes us want to show mercy to ourselves and others. It makes us want to share the message of grace with everyone.

This song, "Amazing Grace," should never be considered a beaten-down, negative view of God, but a soul-rejoicing truth of our undeserved salvation. And that's *super* power. Of course, to experience God's true grace, we must first understand our true condition, which is weakness.

> But he said to me, "My grace is sufficient for you, for my power is made perfect in weakness." Therefore I will boast all the more gladly of my weaknesses, so that the power of Christ may rest upon me. (2 Corinthians 12:9)

So, the next time you sing "Amazing Grace," sing it with overcoming power, but don't leave out the original Source of power—the real Overcomer—Christ Jesus.

> Let us then approach the throne of grace with confidence, so that we may receive mercy and find grace to help us in our time of need. (Hebrews 4:16)

Yes, Scripture states we approach with confidence; however, we move toward that throne to "receive mercy."

Remember standing in front of the firing squad ready to be executed, only to discover you are acquitted? How did you feel right before you heard that someone had forgiven you? You were in need. Down, hurt, weary—insert the word that best describes your pitiful condition. We require God's mercy. Only when we realize that Christ broke the chains are we able to be truly set free.

Grace is not the point where a soul is set free; instead, it's the condition that exists so that, when understood and adhered to, it delivers mercy that breaks those chains and sets someone free.

That's the power of amazing grace.

17

The Power of Single-Mindedness

Have you ever known people with a one-track mind? They tend to drive others crazy by talking about their passion and continually making it the center of attention. Take note, though, because they will accomplish what they set out to do. This is the power behind a one-track mind: single-mindedness.

Jesus was single-minded as He moved toward His purpose, His mission. No one was going to sway Him, even when He was as young as age twelve, when His parents were frantically looking for Him and finally found Him preaching in the Temple.

> When his parents saw him, they were astonished. His mother said to him, "Son, why have you treated us like this? Your father and I have been anxiously searching for you."
>
> "Why were you searching for me?" he asked. "Didn't you know I had to be in my Father's house?" (Luke 2:48–49)

Christ was going about His Father's business. Even up to the night before His execution, in the garden of Gethsemane, He prayed:

> Father, if you are willing, take this cup from me; yet not my will, but yours be done. (Luke 22:42)

I believe that if we want to hear the words, "Well done, good and faithful servant," from our Lord, we must be single-minded. We must not let social, political, or even religious correctness override or compete with spiritual accuracy. Consistently, we want to choose God over people. We must understand that, each day of our lives, we choose whom we will serve. If we don't intentionally make hard decisions daily to be loyal to our Father, we become servants to Satan.

> No one can serve two masters. Either you will hate the one and love the other, or you will be devoted to the one and despise the other. You cannot serve both God and money. (Matthew 6:24)

Single-mindedness doesn't necessarily mean having only one thing on your mind. It means having *one* mind—the mind of Christ. As God's children, we can think like Christ; however, few of us choose to access this most invaluable weapon for battling the enemy. Instead, the modern, so-called Christian today is always compromising, tossed back and forth like a wave in the sea of culture and religious nonsense.

Wisdom is the most significant asset of single-mindedness, but there is one stipulation: We must stay the course and not waver. Waver from what? Check out what James had to say:

> If any of you lacks wisdom, you should ask God, who gives generously to all without finding fault, and it will be given to you. But when you ask, you must believe and not doubt. (James 1:5–6a)

We must not waver in faith. We must believe God's promises. God says that He rewards those who believe, for without faith it's impossible to please God.

> Because the one who doubts is like a wave of the sea, blown and tossed by the wind. That person should not expect to receive

anything from the Lord. Such a person is double-minded and unstable in all they do. (James 1:6b–8)

Single-mindedness means we're willing to trust God all the way, even if it looks like there is no hope and no chance, and even if we've done everything we could. Time has run out, yet we still cling to God. That's when God honors our single-mindedness and delivers us.

We Are What We Think

Single-mindedness brings truth in whatever our minds are focused on. If it's money, then the truth is we love money. If it's career, then the truth is, we're career-minded. It's the same with any worldly desire that supersedes our passion for speaking and living God's truth. The most eye-opening example of double-mindedness in Scripture, along with God's response to it, is in Revelation 3:16, where God says to the church of the Laodiceans, "So, because you are lukewarm—neither hot nor cold—I am about to spit you out of my mouth."

Christ explains that a person is single-minded when he or she is hot or cold. If we're hot (on fire for the truth and seeking to put God first), we are one-minded toward God's things. If we're cold (don't love or care for God or the things of God), then we are single-minded toward the world and the temporary. If we're lukewarm (neither hot nor cold), then we are actually double-minded. Why? The only way to become lukewarm is to mix together hot and cold. Some people may seem to be on fire for God, but they are actually corrupted by the "cares of this world."

But the worries of this life, the deceitfulness of wealth and the desires for other things come in and choke the word, making it unfruitful. (Mark 4:19)

Why would Christ prefer us to be cold instead of lukewarm? A cold person at least has a chance to become hot, but it's hard for a lukewarm person to go either cold or hot. That's what I call a spirit of religion. It's the act of creating a god that fits the agenda of a man-made doctrine.

I know your deeds that you are neither cold nor hot. I wish you were either one or the other! (Revelation 3:15)

Notice that Jesus never says, "If you are cold for me, then I will vomit you out of my mouth." Yes, those who are cold will face judgment and be rejected by God for refusing Him. Still, Jesus is elevating the state of being lukewarm to another level of abomination and heresy. It is foul enough to make our Lord cough in disgust. The lukewarm are not only deceived; they're also deceivers. They're deceived into thinking they have right standing with God. They deceive by providing a false example of the real Christian walk. This double-mindedness is depicted by our Lord as one of the worst conditions of the heart. Lukewarm spirituality essentially means that God cannot coexist with anyone in that condition.

Is Being Double-Minded a Salvation Issue?

It's incredible how we're always trying to find a loophole or an out clause when it comes to God's Word. We want to live as close to the edge of salvation as possible without falling into eternal destruction. I'm sorry to say there is no out clause with God. Either we are single-minded or double-minded; we choose one or the other each day of our existence.

The best way to become single-minded and stay there is to think like God by using our "mind of Christ," exercising our freedom and authority in God's things and not in the matters of this world; we must test the spirits and guard our hearts. The ultimate benefit of being single-minded is that we become elevated to a new enlightenment that the natural person cannot perceive. We receive our master's degree in spiritual understanding.

> The person without the Spirit does not accept the things that come from the Spirit of God but considers them foolish and cannot understand them because they are discerned only through the Spirit. The person with the Spirit makes judgments about all things, but such a person is not subject to merely human judgments, for, "Who has known the mind of the Lord so as to instruct him? But we have the mind of Christ." (1 Corinthians 2:14-16)

This kind of single-mindedness is only experienced by a select few. Many are called, but only a few are chosen to have the mind of our Lord.

18

The Power of Age

"You ain't getting older, you're getting better." I've heard this familiar statement many times throughout the years. Unfortunately, it seldom truthfully applies to humans; usually, only vintage products like wine, antiques, or coins improve with age. Age is a peculiar condition wherein it seems the body starts falling apart, yet the most considerable amount of experience and wisdom belongs to none other than the "aged."

If applied correctly, experience from age nurtures wisdom, and wisdom is the key to success in any area of life.

Proverbs 16:31 illustrates the proper regard for aging:

Gray hair is a crown of splendor; it is attained in the way of righteousness.

The condition here is that age must be found in righteousness; in other words, only a long walk through life with God will bear the fruit of wisdom. Unfortunately, we tend to discount our older generation and give power to the young and beautiful, especially in entertainment and—worst of all—our churches. Hollywood and the entertainment industry have been culprits in this scheme to disrespect the aged and coax the younger generation to follow instead their peers through film, music, dance, and most arts.

But why is this? When we go to a doctor, don't we look for one with experience and wisdom? When we take our cars for repair, don't we go to someone who has been a mechanic for years? Of course we do. So why, then, do we tend to push older generations out of church leadership? Why have Western churches disregarded elders' wisdom in favor of young, handsome, and charismatic smooth-talkers? Youthful, "hip" pastors in skinny jeans attempt to be "seeker-friendly" to the culture. What's disturbing is that the older generation is generally either sparsely scattered among the crowd or sitting way in the back of the sanctuary, having little or no involvement in worship services or in mentoring—other than serving coffee and donuts or handing out bulletins.

Pizza, Games, and a Little "Jesus"

The aim of youth programs in many churches today is to become as much like the popular entertainment restaurants as possible, with a Chuck E. Cheese-type pastor and plenty of pizza and games to draw a crowd. In many cases, young people leading the youth groups are really cases of the blind leading the blind; placing seasoned elders in leadership seems to be an abomination in these seeker-friendly churches. It's even more ridiculous when considering that the very young folks who are going into leadership were only brought up on the Chuck E. Cheese foundation of postmodern "Christianity." Yet, they are expected to be wise shepherds to flocks of souls who need spiritual nourishment and protection. The expectation placed upon these young pastors is to entertain and increase church attendance by planning church retreats and presenting feel-good sermons so the next generation of "pastors" can lead the next generation of youth; this is what they were taught, so they continue to teach it. And the generational curse continues.

Being a leader with true power comes with age and experience. Bible stories about the Flood, the Promised Land, the Great Exodus out of Egypt, and many other topics have one thing in common: in each account, God's people were led by an older person—much older. Moses, Abraham, and Noah are only a few of the wise elders who carried the torch of God's plan and truth to future generations.

Remember the days of old; consider the generations long past. Ask your father and he will tell you, your elders, and they will explain to you. (Deuteronomy 32:7)

We're clearly instructed to heed the wisdom of godly elders. We are called to remember history and seek guidance from those who witnessed it firsthand. Failure to do so only leads to repeating mistakes throughout generations. As we see in the book of Deuteronomy, over and over again, Moses gave the Israelites explicit instructions from God to be careful not to succumb to the pagan ways of the nations they defeated. Further, Moses instructed them to teach God's commands and His people's history to their children and their children's children. This can only be accomplished by having their wisdom, patience, and understanding sculpted by many years of experience, and that's why it is of utmost importance to seek the wisdom of elders.

Better to Be Rebuked by an Elder than by God

The nation of Israel paints a picture of what happens when we fail to listen to elders' wisdom. We lose God's favor and provoke His wrath and discipline.

Do not rebuke an older man harshly, but exhort him as if he were your father. Treat younger men as brothers, older women

as mothers, and younger women as sisters, with absolute purity.
(1 Timothy 5:1–2)

We have veered away from how God intends us to deal with the
aged, and we're suffering for it. The church favors young leaders over
older ones; congregations are spiritually malnourished because they're
not given the solid spiritual food of spiritually seasoned wisdom. The
falling away and complacency are the results of rebelling against God's
love and purpose for our older generation.

Grandpa's Purpose Isn't on the Golf Course

Even when I am old and gray, do not forsake me, my God, till I
declare your power to the next generation, your mighty acts to
all who are to come. (Psalm 71:18)

It's not only the fault of our youth that older folks have been "put out
to pasture," but it's also the generational curse of retirement. The word
"retirement" doesn't even exist in the Bible. Yet the failure of seniors to
show God's strength to the younger generation, therefore not revealing
His power to the generations to come, have caused them to miss out on
fulfilling their multigenerational purpose.

God says the older generation has a designed passion and ability to
lead and mold future generations. As believers grow older, they grow
closer to God because their relationship with Him withstands the test of
time and is strengthened by various trials. They have been brought up
from spiritual youth to spiritual maturity; the result is an increased passion for teaching and leading others to God's glory.

Throw Away That Walker

He gives strength to the weary and increases the power of the weak. (Isaiah 40:29)

When an older person with failing health begins to mentor the younger generations, I've noticed that, miraculously, many become physically able to do God's work—and, yes, many even experience complete healing.

For years, my wife and I have taken our children to sing and play gospel music in retirement homes where the aged walk with canes and move around in wheelchairs or even on stretchers. After getting them involved in our program by clapping and singing songs—and letting them know how valuable they are—we've seen multiple miracles: Many of these older folks have thrown away their canes, ditched their wheelchairs, and even jumped off their stretchers to dance and sing.

While the aged may not have all the physical capabilities of the young, God promises strength to those who seek Him. Whatever a believer's age, God grants the strength to carry out the assigned task. Old age is no reason to stop working or to force someone out of doing God's work. We may retire from our earthly jobs, but God's work is ongoing without excuse. If you are aged and a seasoned believer, then you have more strength and power than any other group in society. Don't allow anyone to tell you otherwise; keep running the race God has set before you with endurance, and continue working for Him, even if it seems like nobody will listen.

Young people, respect your elders; they were once young, too, so they know what you are going through. Someday, you will have the power of age, but only if you first respect those who are going before you. Let's break this generational curse and get God's older generation off the bench and back in the game—and let's watch them score spiritual touchdowns.

That's the power of age.

Plug in to the Power Source

To install electrical hardware, update it, or fix an electrical problem, electricians must first find the source of the power. Why? Because the wiring directly originates from that source so as not to compromise the electrical work or present any danger. Electricians who don't operate from the original power source will do a poor job. Anyone who doesn't respect electrical power (and its deadly consequences) usually ends up badly hurt or even dead. These principles also apply to our spiritual nature; we must understand where our power comes from and who is really in charge.

> I am the vine; you are the branches. If you remain in me and I in you, you will bear much fruit; apart from me you can do nothing. (John 15:5)

God is our only source of power. Without Him, we are powerless; we are nothing. We want to make sure we are plugged into the correct outlet—God's, not Satan's.

Sometimes I plug in my computer at my favorite coffee shop, only to discover that the outlet is dead. God's outlet is never powerless. Satan's outlet is always dead and void of any beneficial power. Scripture tells us that unless we're attached to the vine, we can't bear fruit; we're destined to merely live a fruitless existence.

Good fruit doesn't fall far from the tree. When we're plugged into a live source of power, we will bear fruit.

> But the fruit of the Spirit is love, joy, peace, forbearance, kindness, goodness, faithfulness, gentleness and self-control. Against such things there is no law. (Galatians 5:22–23)

Jesus manifested these fruits, even to the dead religious system that eventually crucified Him. Outwardly, the scribes and Pharisees had an appearance of love for God, but inwardly they were a dead man's bones.

> Woe to you, teachers of the law and Pharisees, you hypocrites! You are like whitewashed tombs, which look beautiful on the outside but on the inside are full of the bones of the dead and everything unclean. (Matthew 23:27)

What is the most potent fruit of all? Love—plain and simple. If we, as God's people, don't show love, then we have nothing at all. It doesn't matter how many college degrees we have hanging on our wall, how big our church is, how many healings we've done, or how many homeless people we've fed. Without love, we have no power, because it's love that fuels the engine. Love is the crucial element for power to even exist.

> Though I speak with the tongues of men and of angels, but have not love, I have become sounding brass or a clanging cymbal.

And though I have the gift of prophecy, and understand all mysteries and all knowledge, and though I have all faith, so that I could remove mountains, but have not love, I am nothing. And though I bestow all my goods to feed the poor, and though I give my body to be burned, but have not love, it profits me nothing. (I Corinthians 13:1–3)

Scripture says we have nothing without love. But what is love? What is the fuel that powers us?

Love is patient, love is kind. It does not envy, it does not boast, it is not proud. It does not dishonor others, it is not self-seeking, it is not easily angered, it keeps no record of wrongs. Love does not delight in evil but rejoices with the truth. It always protects, always trusts, always hopes, always perseveres. (1 Corinthians 13:4–7)

We often think of God's power displayed through miracles, healing, and casting out demons, but love is the what and why behind those supernatural deeds. Love is the reason we do these acts of power. It's love that makes sense of it all. So now that we know that the reason behind our power—I should say God's power—is love, let's move forward in our purpose. Jesus told us in Matthew 10:7–8:

As you go, proclaim this message: "The kingdom of heaven has come near." Heal the sick, raise the dead, cleanse those who have leprosy, drive out demons. Freely you have received; freely give.

What are some manifestations of love?

Prayer

When we truly love, we are concerned about others. One way to reflect that concern is by praying for them. We communicate with the Father, asking for blessings, healing, deliverance, protection, and wisdom for others in Jesus' name. If we're plugged into the source of power, we will have power in our prayers.

> Therefore confess your sins to each other and pray for each other so that you may be healed. The prayer of a righteous person is powerful and effective. (James 5:16)

Forgiveness

If we are plugged into the source of power, we will be able to offer forgiveness to those who have wronged us.

> And when you stand praying, if you hold anything against anyone, forgive them, so that your Father in heaven may forgive you your sins. (Mark 11:25)

Patience

If we are plugged into the source of power, we will have divine patience to weather whatever trials we face.

> Being strengthened with all power according to his glorious might so that you may have great endurance and patience, and giving joyful thanks to the Father, who has qualified you to share

in the inheritance of his holy people in the kingdom of light. (Colossians 1:11–12)

Wisdom

If we are plugged into the source of power, we will have wisdom.

For the Lord gives wisdom; from his mouth come knowledge and understanding. (Proverbs 2:6)

Our Purpose

If we are plugged into the source of power, we will find and understand our purpose.

He has saved us and called us to a holy life—not because of anything we have done but because of his own purpose and grace. This grace was given us in Christ Jesus before the beginning of time. (2 Timothy 1:9)

Love is the most excellent fruit; it's time to have a fruitful harvest. If we are plugged into the source of power, we will experience a fruitful harvest. Jesus is the "Lord of the harvest," and He tells us that "the harvest is great, but the workers are few" (Luke 10:2). So it's time to grasp our purpose by getting out into that field. Will you fulfill your purpose by being one of the chosen?

That's the power of plugging into the right source.

The Power of Living in the Supernatural

Years ago, I arrived in Hollywood with no money, no film degree, no industry connections. The only asset I had to my name was the passion for doing what I felt God was calling me to do. To date I have written, directed, starred in, and distributed more than fifty feature films. Over the years, numerous people have asked me how I made so many movies outside of the "Hollywood system." When I explain that it has been supernatural—a miracle from God—they immediately reply, "Yes, but show us *how* you did it." How do you show someone how God does something, other than to mark it up as a miracle—a supernatural intervention into the natural? So, no matter how many times I give this answer, I receive the same response. They don't hear me say, "God did it"; they want a "legit" explanation. There isn't *anything* I can say that will convince them of the supernatural miracle God has performed in my life. They want a sign.

In Mark 8, we read that Jesus fed thousands of hungry people with a few loaves of bread and a few fish. He performed a miracle that would bring any truth-seeker to his or her knees in worship of God. Afterward, however, the Pharisees came to Christ, asking for a sign; they wanted *more* proof—a *better* miracle than He had performed.

> About four thousand were present. After he had sent them away, he got into the boat with his disciples and went to the region of Dalmanutha.

The Pharisees came and began to question Jesus. To test him, they asked him for a sign from heaven. He sighed deeply and said, "Why does this generation ask for a sign? Truly I tell you, no sign will be given to it." (Mark 8:9–12)

God looks at the heart, and if that heart seeks a sign to validate whether He is God, then most likely, no sign will be given. God wants a spirit that's hungry for Him. If we approach Him as children with believing hearts, God may reveal a sign, such as a healing, a deliverance, or an unexplainable event.

One of the biggest mistakes Christians make is thinking that God measures us based on our education, background, spiritual gifts, or ability to quote and analyze Scripture; however, that kind of thinking can be a stumbling block to true faith, as we see in Mark 8.

"Do you have eyes but fail to see, and ears but fail to hear? And don't you remember? When I broke the five loaves for the five thousand, how many basketfuls of pieces did you pick up?"

"Twelve," they replied.

"And when I broke the seven loaves for the four thousand, how many basketfuls of pieces did you pick up?"

They answered, "Seven."

He said to them, "Do you still not understand?"
(Mark 8:18–21)

If I were Jesus, I would've been frustrated with the disciples. Then, they mentioned that they had forgotten bread. Instead of replying, Jesus stated that the religious people were a stumbling block to the Gospel. After the disciples had witnessed Christ's miracle of feeding thousands from the meager supplies, they freaked out because they hadn't brought enough food. I wonder if Jesus felt frustrated that food was an issue. Food is not an issue when we believe in the supernatural.

Jesus told them that they didn't need to worry about having enough food. He had created a meal for thousands, multiplying what was already there. Yet they were hung up on not having enough in the flesh, and they completely missed the point Jesus was trying to teach them: No matter how many miracles He did, few believed the miracles were real or that they could be repeated.

Isn't this just like humans today? Even in the Christian community, many of us receive answers to prayers and witness miracle after miracle. Yet, our faith seems to remain like that of the disciples—more focused on the natural rather than the supernatural. Neither the disciples nor the Pharisees understood supernatural matters. This is where God lives and operates, yet we keep going right back to the natural realm and focusing on the situation as it seems to be, instead of believing that God is dealing with our problems supernaturally.

As eternal spirit beings living in mortal bodies maneuvering through the natural world (1 Corinthians 15:53), we find it difficult not to keep slipping back into the "worrying about provision" or "give me a sign" mentality. We should remember that God is continuously working His way in our lives for good (Romans 8:28), and He always has our back (Deuteronomy 3:22).

It may seem hopeless on occasion, but those times are when we have the opportunity to please the Father by exercising our faith. Remember, the supernatural is seen only with spiritual eyes, and unless we continuously view our problems through spiritual eyes, we will inevitably depend on the natural. Faith does not—and cannot—thrive in a world where things are seen only with the natural eye.

Now faith is confidence in what we hope for and assurance about what we do not see. (Hebrews 11:1)

That's the power of living in the supernatural.

The Power of Good Ground

Do not be deceived: God cannot be mocked. A man reaps
what he sows. Whoever sows to please their flesh,
from the flesh will reap destruction; whoever sows to
please the Spirit, from the Spirit will reap eternal life.

GALATIANS 6:7–8

Throughout God's Word, planting and harvesting metaphorically explain ideas surrounding good, evil, money, love, salvation, and other kingdom principles. Soil sometimes refers to the condition of our heart, and our Lord considers this perhaps the cornerstone of our eternal destiny.

Soil has also been of utmost importance to humanity throughout history; mankind has relied on good ground to survive. From the early to mid-1830s, the Oregon Trail was used by about four hundred thousand settlers who uprooted their lives in the East, risking their lives by going West to find deep, dark, fertile soil. Dirt is essential to farmers because that's what makes seeds grow, yielding a good crop. Jesus also valued good soil of the soul; He used it to explain how faith and eternal life played out in the kingdom of heaven, as we see in Matthew 13:3–8:

Then he told them many things in parables, saying: "A farmer went out to sow his seed. As he was scattering the seed, some fell along the path, and the birds came and ate it up. Some fell on rocky places, where it did not have much soil. It sprang up quickly because the soil was shallow. But when the sun came up, the plants were scorched, and they withered because they had no root. Other seed fell among thorns, which grew up and choked the plants. Still other seed fell on good soil, where it produced a crop—a hundred, sixty or thirty times what was sown."

The settlers were seeking fertile soil because only good soil can produce a good crop. In this passage, Christ conveys the importance of having such a commitment to our faith that our good soil remains good and continues to produce good fruit—this is the power of good soil. When the condition of a good-soil heart is right, then all kinds of benefits manifest, from having the power to cast out demons and heal the sick to being able to speak boldly for God and, most important of all, having the power to love. Yes, as explained in the passage of Scripture below, the most important fruit of all that grows from good ground is love; without it, soil is worthless.

Power of the Fruit

But the fruit of the Spirit is love, joy, peace, forbearance, kindness, goodness, faithfulness, gentleness, and self-control. Against such things there is no law. Those who belong to Christ Jesus have crucified the flesh with its passions and desires. Since we live by the Spirit, let us keep in step with the Spirit. (Galatians 5:22–25)

The fruit produced by walking in the Spirit empowers us to do good works.

The Key That Unlocks the Power of Good Soil

A Christian's good soil will yield much fruit:

> But the seed falling on good soil refers to someone who hears the word and understands it. This is the one who produces a crop, yielding a hundred, sixty or thirty times what was sown. (Matthew 13:23)

Here's a central scriptural truth that's often overlooked: Jesus says that the good ground represents those who hear the Word of God and understand it. Hearing the Word of God is only *part* of what it means to be good soil; one must *understand* it. The conundrum is, "Does the Word of God create good soil, or does the Word of God only grow in good soil?" Good soil is the heart's condition; it's not measured by knowledge of Scripture, performing good deeds, or even being righteous. Instead, it is the willingness to allow God's Word to take root and grow, and that's when knowing Scripture becomes understanding, and the good deeds become acceptable to God. That's when we become right with our Lord, birthing righteousness. People are categorized by the type of ground that's conducive to growth. When the seed (the Word of God) unites with their soil condition, that dictates growth. The key is what is produced (or not produced) when the seed is planted. Notice that all the soil types hear and receive the Word, but only one type of soil yields fruit. Therefore, the Word of God doesn't create good soil; it grows in good soil.

I asked a successful farmer his most significant challenge in maintaining healthy soil. "Contamination," he responded. "When soil is contaminated, it is extremely difficult for the crop to grow, and it becomes harmful to humans living on it or near it." What contaminates soil? "Soil contaminants are all products of pollutants that destroy the soil: human activities, pesticide chemicals, urban or industrial waste, or radioactive emissions," he explained. Wow! The main reason for contamination is human intervention. Spiritually speaking, the world is what contaminates our soil.

> Let us not become weary in doing good, for at the proper time
> we will reap a harvest if we do not give up. (Galatians 6:9)

The power of our soil is determined not only by being proactive but by being reactive. This means that we need to continually discern the spirits regarding who and what is around our soil. The demons know that if they can contaminate a child of God's soil, it is easier to take down that child.

The quality of our soil's ingredients depends not only on conditioning the soil, but primarily on protecting it. As God's elect in these last days, we realize that the devil will try many strategies to take souls to hell. He knows his time is short. We must protect our soil—our heart—lest we become as what Christ described in Matthew 13:22:

> The seed falling among the thorns refers to someone who hears
> the word, but the worries of this life and the deceitfulness of
> wealth choke the word, making it unfruitful.

Satan is always there to offer us a tasty dish of sin (often when we least expect it) through money, power, or lust, which births addiction and becomes a vicious cycle. That fruit will eventually rot. But, praise God, we overcome, and our garden grows as we pray for one another and remain humble and thankful.

What is the manifestation of our fruit? Souls. Again, Matthew 13:23 says:

> But the seed falling on good soil refers to someone who hears the
> word and understands it. This is the one who produces a crop,
> yielding a hundred, sixty or thirty times what was sown.

It's time for God's people to produce fruit so the Gospel is preached throughout the world.

That's the ultimate power of good ground.

Power in These Last Days

Do not conform to the pattern of this world, but be
transformed by the renewing of your mind.
Then you will be able to test and approve what God's will is—
his good, pleasing and perfect will.

Romans 12:2

If we watched life as if it were a movie, these last days would be viewed as a scene in which good battles evil. We'd be sitting on the edge of our seats. The film makes us think the bad guys will win, but we know that the good guys will, because we've read the book (the Bible), and we know that's how it ends.

As God's elect, we're the characters in that movie fighting that battle, as outlined in Matthew 24:7–12:

Nation will rise against nation, and kingdom against kingdom. There will be famines and earthquakes in various places. All these are the beginning of birth pains. Then you will be handed over to be persecuted and put to death, and you will be hated by all nations because of me. At that time many will turn away from the faith and will betray and hate each other, and many false prophets will appear and deceive many people. Because of the increase of wickedness, the love of most will grow cold.

Wow! If this were a real movie, it would be cinema at its best, a true epic, putting to shame even films such as *Ben Hur*, *The Ten Commandments*, and *Gone with the Wind*. It seems that the protagonists, you and I, don't stand a fighting chance, and evil will prevail, but praise God, we know exactly how this movie ends. Still, the war is brutal, and the trials include pain, suffering, and loss. No matter the cost, however, we stay in the battle.

Search and Rescue

For who do we search? Whom do we rescue? We seek out the lost—those who don't know Christ. We preach the good news of salvation. Our task is to testify in order to rescue them from perishing in hell.

The Lord is not slow in keeping his promise, as some understand slowness. Instead he is patient with you, not wanting anyone to perish, but everyone to come to repentance. (2 Peter 3:9)

The *Titanic* is rapidly sinking, time is running out, and God is waiting mercifully for more sinners to repent.

The second focus of our search and rescue is God's remnant—His elect. They're either battling on their own in some undisclosed location, they're prisoners of the enemy needing encouragement, or they're simply not yet awakened to the battle. As God's frontline warriors, we are commissioned to attack and defeat the enemy to restore fellow believers.

Power Tools

Test the Spirits

> Dear friends, do not believe every spirit, but test the spirits to see whether they are from God, because many false prophets have gone out into the world. This is how you can recognize the Spirit of God: Every spirit that acknowledges that Jesus Christ has come in the flesh is from God, but every spirit that does not acknowledge Jesus is not from God. This is the spirit of the antichrist, which you have heard is coming and even now is already in the world. (1 John 4:1–3)

In these times, we must always test the spirits. The devil is roaming around to seek whom he can devour; as mentioned already, because he knows his time is short, he ramps up his attack. Since what we see in the physical realm can be deceiving, we always look at things from the spiritual viewpoint. And, we take time to listen.

The number-one problem with many Christians today is that our mouths are bigger than our ears. Most churches teach Christians to go out and preach and give their ears a siesta. Meanwhile, the devil is having a party with addiction, perversion, and every kind of evil, dividing and conquering the very souls we're trying to reach. True preaching is not a one-way street. It's a double-lane highway, with one lane for speaking and the other for listening. A truly effective evangelist should be able to walk into any room and test the spirits by first listening and then speaking, because the devil will always expose himself when there is silence. We need to spend more time on our knees before God, getting our instruction, and less time flapping our jaws. If we listen long enough, the devil slips up and exposes himself. Prayer allows us to see through the devil's tactics and understand how to deal with them. Most people pray and rush into life without taking time to listen for God's input on how to respond.

Be Watchful

We should always watch for the type of fruit people yield; we identify God's children by the loving righteousness they bear.

> By their fruit you will recognize them. Do people pick grapes from thornbushes, or figs from thistles? Likewise, every good tree bears good fruit, but a bad tree bears bad fruit. A good tree cannot bear bad fruit, and a bad tree cannot bear good fruit. (Matthew 7:16–18)

When we watch, God's Holy Spirit within us reveals whether a person is of God.

First Thessalonians 5:21 (KJV) commands:

> Prove all things; hold fast that which is good.

Use Your Mind of Christ

We have the mind of Christ and we need to act on it. In reality, we can think and behave like Christ.

> "Who has known the mind of the Lord so as to instruct him?" But we have the mind of Christ. (1 Corinthians 2:16)

When we dwell in the presence of God and the presence of God dwells in us, we have the mind of Christ. We can have the upper hand over the enemy.

Take Action

Faith without works is dead.

As the body without the spirit is dead, so faith without deeds is dead. (James 2:26)

Territories that the enemy has taken over can be taken back, but only with spiritual warfare.

You, dear children, are from God and have overcome them because the one who is in you is greater than the one who is in the world. (1 John 4:4)

Sometimes we have to be the hands and feet of Christ. We shouldn't think that because we're "prayed up," we can sit and watch while the rest of the Body of Christ fights the battle for us. Like actors in Hollywood epic films, we may feel like we're always facing an unbeatable giant, a hopeless and impossible task. We must remember that, with God, all things are possible—but only when we remain alert, on guard, and ready to take action according to the guiding of the Holy Spirit.

But the Advocate, the Holy Spirit, whom the Father will send in my name, will teach you all things and will remind you of everything I have said to you. (John 14:26)

That's the true power God equips us with during this final hour.

The Power of Creating Something from Nothing

As a filmmaker, the question I'm asked most often is, "What if I don't have the money to make my movie?" I love the movie *Field of Dreams*; in it, actor Kevin Costner hears a voice saying, "Build it, and they will come." Build what? Your dream. We must first understand how God has programmed us. Since God created us in His image, we have an undeniable, innate desire to imitate Him by being creative. Perhaps the creation of mankind and this universe is the most brilliant low-budget indie film of all time. God took nothing and made something.

Maybe this is God's filmmaking formula:

1. God created the world in six days (a quick shooting schedule).
2. The world sure was beautiful (but it was simple).
3. There was one location (the Garden of Eden).
4. The wardrobe was inexpensive (just a leaf or two).
5. There were only three characters (Adam, Eve, and the antagonist Satan).
6. The plot is simple (man meets woman and falls in love, woman falls for snake and eats the apple, and, well, it's been the longest-running soap opera in history).

Even God started simply. No matter what we have in front of us, whether it's a mountain that seems unclimbable or the Red Sea that appears uncrossable, understand that God is there. The force that created the world from nothing is the same force within us today. Let's talk about some elements of creating something from nothing.

Prayer

The first key element is prayer.

> "Have faith in God," Jesus answered. "Truly I tell you, if anyone says to this mountain, 'Go, throw yourself into the sea,' and does not doubt in their heart but believes that what they say will happen, it will be done for them. Therefore I tell you, whatever you ask for in prayer, believe that you have received it, and it will be yours." (Mark 11:22–24)

Christ focuses on prayer; He tells us that we already have the power to overcome when we face an obstacle. Whenever He calls us to create, we usually encounter physical, emotional, or spiritual barriers. We forget, though, that we are spiritual beings having a human experience, so we turn to man's ideas and logic. We don't seek the supernatural, which is where God lives and creates. Therefore, we must move out of the physical and into the spiritual. The only way is through prayer. Prayer conditions the heart; it does not conform God to our will. Prayer does not move God, but prayer does move us. However, prayer alone is not enough.

Faith

The passage cited above says we're not to doubt, and that we're to combine belief with our prayers. When we stop doubting and start believing, we have faith. To sum it up, prayer moves us—through faith.

Scripture provides many accounts of people who have great faith. Here are three:

The woman who needed healing: A woman who had been sick with an issue of blood for years with no hope of healing navigated her way through a crowd to touch Christ's robe. He felt the power go out of Him, and told her that her faith had made her whole (see Luke 8:43–48).

The centurion whose servant needed healing: A centurion approached Christ from a distance and asked that He heal his servant. Jesus was willing to go to the soldier's house, but the soldier told Jesus that he was not worthy for Jesus to come to him; all Jesus had to do was to speak the word and the servant would be healed. Christ, amazed at the centurion's faith, spoke the word, and the servant was healed (see Matthew 8:5–13).

The woman whose demon-possessed daughter needed healing: A Gentile woman went to Jesus and asked Him to heal her demon-possessed daughter. Jesus told the woman that He did not come to heal anyone who wasn't Jewish, and He used the example of "dogs" (referring to pets). The woman replied, "But even the dogs eat the crumbs that fall off the table onto the floor." When Christ heard what she said, He was so impressed that He healed her daughter after telling the woman, "You have great faith" (see Matthew 15:21–28).

Yes, faith is vital. However, without the next component, all the faith in the world will not help.

Forgiveness

And when you stand praying, if you hold anything against any-one, forgive them, so that your Father in heaven may forgive you your sins. (Mark 11:25–26)

Wow! This point is often overlooked and not preached today—no wonder the church is impotent. Unless we forgive, we can't move forward, because hurt becomes unforgiveness, and unforgiveness gives birth to anger. This scenario is played out through the arts, particularly through music, film, and television.

No matter what genre, whether it's rock, pop, rap, or country, we hear many stories of brokenness and even anger in the lyrics of music. All this stems from unforgiveness. I don't mean every song needs to be about a perfect or restored life, but much of today's music is downright demonic. It's dark, and proudly exhibits rage against anything of God and His truth.

Have you ever watched a movie and wondered how anyone could produce, much less write, themes so dark and hopeless—and seem to take pleasure in doing it? I've not only seen this being done, but I've been one of the filmmakers who has done it. Why? Because most artists, whether filmmakers, musicians, actors, or painters, come from a place of brokenness. Many times, someone has injured them, and they're carrying loads of unforgiven hurt. They attempt to deal with it through their art. Unfortunately, those who listen to or watch these reflections are sucked into the broken world of this bitter hurt and unforgiveness, which only breeds more anger and unforgiveness. It's a vicious cycle.

Since we're made in our Heavenly Father's image (and He is the Master Designer who created something out of nothing), we can create and design like our Father. Remember, we came into this world with nothing, and we'll leave with the same. Everything that takes place between our birth and death is what we do with the time we're here. While we're here, God gives us the time and tools to create anything out of nothing. Now, it's one thing to create something that tells a story of brokenness (this is the Gospel of salvation), but we must do it from a place of healing to maintain a balance and not spew Satan's rhetoric.

Vision

Think of your creativity as a giant engine, the motor that drives your project to fruition. Let's call the engine your vision. Your idea doesn't need to be crystal clear or even detailed enough to fully explain it. God knows your vision, and He's the only one who really counts, because He's the one behind it. Start with your image, and even if it's not logical, explainable, or barely readable, it's ok. Write it down.

> Then the Lord replied: "Write down the revelation and make it plain on tablets so that a herald may run with it." (Habakkuk 2:2)

As time progresses, your vision will become more apparent. When God gave me the script for *The Last Evangelist*, I didn't know why I was writing it or what I would do with it! I was a full-time evangelist; I wasn't making films like I had been doing in the past. But still, God implanted the idea within me to use my filmmaking talent for His glory. Next, He gave me the final ingredient.

Passion

The fuel that powers the engine is passion. Without passion, we cannot succeed. It's what God had when He sent His Son to live and die for us. He had passion. His intention was to show love; love is a voice above all others. The devotion of Christ led Him to fulfill His destiny that the Father intended. Jesus' passion was His love for the Father, revealed by doing His will.

The Father gives us the power to create as He does. When we use that power, we create either for or against God. We cannot serve God and man. We must choose who we create something from nothing for.

Then we experience the power of creating.

The Power of Fearing the Lord

> Praise the Lord. Blessed are those who fear the Lord,
> who find great delight in his commands.
>
> PSALM 112:1

The lack of fear of the Lord is the core reason for today's watered-down religious system; when people don't fear God, they think they don't need to repent.

"Repent? Why? I didn't do anything wrong. Oh, that's like old-time religion stuff. Don't you know about grace? It abounds for all. We are under grace—so there's no need to come crying to God. Jesus has done the work on the cross."

This is the biggest lie put forward by today's counterfeit churches, leading the vulnerable straight to hell. The main reason for not fearing God is a lack of respect, and respect starts with understanding who God is and what He requires. When you're in the presence of God, you're standing on holy ground. Have you ever entered someone's house and they ask you to remove your shoes? Out of respect, you do it, no questions asked. Isn't it sad that more emphasis is put on keeping carpets clean than honoring God's holy ground?

Tremble, earth, at the presence of the Lord, at the presence of the God of Jacob. (Psalm 114:7)

One of the things we must learn to do is tremble. There are various reasons we might tremble, ranging from anxiety and fright to intense terror. Modern religion misinterprets "fear" to mean "scared or paranoid"; however, we are really talking about spiritual fear. This kind of fear encompasses our whole being—body, mind, and soul. Biblically, "fear" is defined as "respect."

Recall the centurion we looked at in a previous chapter, whose servant was on the brink of death (see again Matthew 8:8–10). Understanding that the soldier's "great faith" was a result of biblical fear and respect for God, we must also realize that his story gives us a lesson about working through our salvation.

Therefore, my dear friends, as you have always obeyed—not only in my presence, but now much more in my absence—continue to work out your salvation with fear and trembling. (Philippians 2:12)

Paul says that obedience is not only a result of fearing the Lord, but it's also qualification for and proof of salvation. Was the centurion saved? I think the question is instead whether he was obedient. Was he fearful of Christ? Did he use faith? I'd say yes, but we must understand that the soldier couldn't have achieved anything without first fearing and respecting God.

Wow! If only we had this kind of fear, what a difference it would make! This centurion soldier certainly was a success in his own right, and it would seem that since he built a synagogue for the Jews, he would have the confidence to approach the King of the Jews Himself. However, the powerful man feared Christ (with respect and reverence), knowing that humans have no place near the God of the Universe. When Christ died and arose for us, we were granted the right to sit with Him at the Father's right hand. However, this doesn't mean we no longer fear or respect God.

On the contrary, we fear Him more than ever with our new self. This fear is the power we need to battle the enemy. Using our authority and power doesn't exempt us from showing God the utmost honor and reverence. Let's look again at how the centurion handled his understanding of power and authority as he spoke to Jesus. He said:

> Lord, I do not deserve to have you come under my roof. But just say the word, and my servant will be healed. For I myself am a man under authority, with soldiers under me. I tell this one, "Go," and he goes; and that one, "Come," and he comes. I say to my servant, "Do this," and he does it. (Matthew 8:8–9)

The soldier understood the chain of command and how to approach a real King and His throne: with fear and trembling through humility and the spoken word. The centurion was preaching the Gospel to Jesus (perhaps without knowing or fully understanding it). He was explaining the way authority works and that through speaking the word, miracles happen. Miracles cannot occur without the fear of God. I love Christ's reaction upon hearing the respectful centurion speaking about authority. Jesus essentially tells the crowd following him, "Here is the winner of the 'fear God' competition. You all are of the 'chosen' race; however, you don't really understand and use the tools the Father has given you, but this 'outsider' gets it."

I believe the amount of power issued to us is really measured by the extent of honor and respect we show our Lord. This can be achieved only by first and foremost fearing the Lord. Anything short of falling on our faces and bowing before God is a failure to defeat the enemy, and that's why it's so important to understand the power of fear.

Reverence unlocks true power!

Power over Satan

Power over Satan is one of the most challenging concepts for those who do not understand their *position* in the Body of Christ and their inheritance of *authority and power* from our Lord. Why? Simple! They don't understand the Scriptures and the power of God. But wait, didn't these preachers and scholars of the Bible graduate with high honors from major Bible colleges, and haven't they diligently studied the Bible? Yes, but few really understand it, so they can't really understand the power of God. Jesus thanked the Father for hiding the precious truth from the "wise."

> At that time Jesus, full of joy through the Holy Spirit, said, "I praise you, Father, Lord of heaven and earth, because you have hidden these things from the wise and learned, and revealed them to little children. Yes, Father, for this is what you were pleased to do." (Luke 10:21)

What was going on at this point to cause Christ to say this? A group of seventy had just returned from spreading the Gospel, and Jesus told them:

The seventy-two returned with joy and said, "Lord, even the demons submit to us in your name."

He replied, "I saw Satan fall like lightning from heaven. I have given you authority to trample on snakes and scorpions and to overcome all the power of the enemy; nothing will harm you." (Luke 10:17–19)

Christ explained that these babes understood and utilized the power of God in a way the religious elite had never conceived. They were battling demonic forces victoriously. Jesus assured them that no force, by any means, would overcome them. To really comprehend the battle between Christ and Satan, though, we need to go to the first time recorded in Scripture where Jesus encountered the devil while He was in the flesh:

Jesus, full of the Holy Spirit, left the Jordan and was led by the Spirit into the wilderness, where for forty days he was tempted by the devil. He ate nothing during those days, and at the end of them he was hungry.

The devil said to him, "If you are the Son of God, tell this stone to become bread." (Luke 4:1–3)

We try our best to live for God by praying, reading Scripture, and even fasting, thinking that's when we're most shielded from evil, but it's actually the opposite. We're only a high-level threat to the enemy when we are closest to our Heavenly Father, like when Satan tempted Jesus. This is why, when we're at our highest peak with God, we're prime targets for Satan. In this story, God shows how to deal with Satan as Jesus did.

The devil led him up to a high place and showed him in an instant all the kingdoms of the world. And he said to him, "I will give you all their authority and splendor; it has been given to me, and I can give it to anyone I want to. If you worship me, it will all be yours."

Jesus answered, "It is written: 'Worship the Lord your God and serve him only.'" (Luke 4:5–8)

Notice that Jesus says, "Worship the Lord your God and serve him only." We must serve only one Master. We serve with single-heartedness, no double-mindedness, having only one mind—the mind of Christ.

Three times the devil went to Jesus to tempt Him:

1. To satisfy our Lord's hunger.
2. To give Jesus anything He wanted in the realm of worldly power and position.
3. To get Christ to defy natural laws in order to force His Father to perform supernaturally in the physical realm.

In each case, Jesus responded immediately with "it is written," proclaiming God's Word to Satan. When a real child of God encounters a demon, the first thing we must do is state God's Word. What is the Word of God? His Son Jesus. When I command a demon to leave, the key words that always come from my mouth are "in the name of Jesus."

Notice that in each instance, Satan offers Jesus something for *Jesus' own* benefit, not for the benefit of others. We can never use our power for our own benefit. I don't mean that we can't command a demon to leave our presence, whether it be from our house or neighborhood; casting out demons from our own presence is certainly beneficial to us! I mean that we must never put God's power on display as a spectacle or use it for personal, financial, or religious gain.

When Satan asked Christ to turn the stone into bread so He could eat it, Christ resisted. Likewise, we shouldn't use the power of miracles for personal satisfaction or worldly wealth.

The next few verses show how Jesus handled the issue of "tempting God," which many believers today are guilty of doing.

> The devil led him to Jerusalem and had him stand on the highest point of the temple. "If you are the Son of God," he said, "throw yourself down from here. For it is written: 'He will command his angels concerning you to guard you carefully; they will lift you up in their hands, so that you will not strike your foot against a stone.'" Jesus answered, "It is said: 'Do not put the Lord your God to the test.'" (Luke 4:9–12)

The devil tried to make our Lord do something that would defy the natural laws God had created. The devil wanted the Father to counter the action of Jesus and perform supernaturally, just as a clown would perform in a circus, giving cheap entertainment to a crowd. I've heard many Christians say that they will do something dangerous, and they don't even worry about it because they claim God is taking care of them. This is nonsense and could get them injured or killed! We should never misuse our God-given gifts by ignoring the laws of nature. Testing God to intervene for no other reason than to prove He is paying attention or to create a "Disneyland experience" is sinful and, quite plainly, absurd. Do not misconstrue the statement in Luke 10:19 that "nothing shall by any means hurt you." This only applies in the proper context. And, speaking of context, another of Satan's tactics is taking Scripture out of context in order to deceive. When Satan was tempting Jesus, he said:

> For it is written: "He will command his angels concerning you to guard you carefully; they will lift you up in their hands, so that you will not strike your foot against a stone." (Luke 4:10–11)

Wow! It's scary to hear the father of lies quote God's Word, but he does, and sometimes his delivery is better than that of most believers.

So, how does this apply today? Remember, Satan is never going to deliver God's Word for the benefit of the Body of Christ. He always uses it for his own advantage. Therefore, he takes God's Word out of context. Sadly, we can walk into many churches and hear a sermon with Scripture taken out of context. Many modern-day preachers have a story that they need to tell based upon what the congregation wants to hear, so they cherry-pick a verse or two to fit their agenda. It's usually a self-help or humanitarian theme. Many religious leaders today spoon feed Satan's carefully crafted lies to their congregations; some leaders are being deceived by good intentions, and others are doing so for personal gain.

We may assume that we lower our chances of encountering the devil again each time we gain a victory over him. This is a misconception, as we see in Luke 4:13:

> When the devil had finished all this tempting, he left him until an opportune time.

The phrase "until an opportune time" points out that the father of lies is always there, waiting for his prey. We all have seasons in our lives, and each one is on a different plane spiritually. We mustn't be deceived into thinking that because we go to church, we're safe. Let's look further into Luke 4.

> In the synagogue there was a man possessed by a demon, an impure spirit. He cried out at the top of his voice, "Go away! What do you want with us, Jesus of Nazareth? Have you come to destroy us? I know who you are—the Holy One of God!"
>
> "Be quiet!" Jesus said sternly. "Come out of him!" Then the demon threw the man down before them all and came out without injuring him. (Luke 4:33–35)

Yes, in a house of God there sits a devil! This wasn't too long after Christ's encounter with Satan in the desert. Just as demons were present when Jesus entered houses of worship, so the evil one dwells within the walls of most churches today. Believer, be aware, be assertive, and be ready to deal with the sins of hell, like our Savior, who is an example for us.

Never make casting out demons a deliverance event, a show of force, or a carnival of sensationalism. In my opinion, that's committing the sin of tempting God. This is serious warfare, and we are victorious only when we understand and adequately use the true power that God has given us. Never think that anyone has a unique ability or ordination to operate in the supernatural. This ability is available to all of God's children; there is no corner on the market for engaging in spiritual warfare. Only God provides the power; nothing and nobody else can do that. Use this power wisely, and remember what Jesus said to the seventy who came back raving about how "even the demons obeyed us" (Luke 10:17).

> However, do not rejoice that the spirits submit to you, but rejoice that your names are written in heaven. (Luke 10:20)

Now I'd say that having our name written in the Book of Life is the ultimate proof of our power over Satan.

26

The Power of the Watch Warrior

The term "prayer warrior" denotes a soul who is in deep, constant communion with the Father, interceding and asking Him for wisdom, protection, healing, guidance, and provision. Scripture tells us to pray continually without ceasing, with supplication and thankfulness. Throughout Scripture, however, God also calls His people to *watch*. Actually, He *warns* us to watch. He sends *watch warriors* who have a heart for God's people to inform them about how current events align with Scripture. The watch warriors are not to be ignored; their purpose in these last days is not only to sound the alarm but to proclaim the truth!

> But about that day or hour no one knows, not even the angels in heaven, nor the Son, but only the Father. Be on guard! Be alert! You do not know when that time will come. (Mark 13:32–33)

Christ has clearly told us that neither the day nor the hour is known to anyone, not even to Jesus Himself, but only the Father; therefore, we need to pray and watch. The watch warrior's job is of utmost importance because the watchman is also considered the doorkeeper.

It's like a man going away: He leaves his house and puts his servants in charge, each with their assigned task, and tells the one at the door to keep watch. (Mark 13:34)

Doorkeepers are the first to see who enters and exits the house; they are responsible for discerning who should come in. We, as God's children, are called to the same task of discerning the spirits. Are they from God or from Satan?

In Matthew 24:4, Jesus stressed this critical point to His disciples when He said, "Watch out that no one deceives you." He told us to be on high alert for last-days deception as the Antichrist prepares to move against God's people.

Though being a "watchman" may not be one of the gifts of the Spirit, it is clear that certain people have excellent skills when it comes to watching. These people seem to have a vision into culture, circumstances, and events that correlate with Scripture. However, in these last days, God is calling all members of His Body to watch.

Some say, "My job isn't being a watchman—I have a different gift." Um, sorry, but that just won't fly, and if you need solid proof, just read this:

Therefore keep watch because you do not know when the owner of the house will come back—whether in the evening, or at midnight, or when the rooster crows, or at dawn. If he comes suddenly, do not let him find you sleeping. What I say to you, I say to everyone: "Watch!" (Mark 13:35–37)

Last time I checked, "everyone" meant "all," and that includes you and me! Being a watchman isn't so much a gift as it is a duty, no matter what our gift may be, whether it's preaching, teaching, prophesying, or whatever. Our duty is to watch! Besides, how could we possibly utilize our spiritual gifts properly if we don't monitor and accurately discern what we see? The simple answer is that we cannot.

How many people are really listening to the watch warriors, much less supporting and encouraging them? The church sometimes puts watch warriors in categories such as fear-mongerers, doomsayers, politically incorrect, culturally irrelevant, or offensive. Perhaps you feel an urgent desire to tell people that what they're doing isn't correct, or you feel compelled to warn them because, based on the fruit they bear, their faith appears to be counterfeit. Maybe you watch the news, then read a passage from Scripture—and bam! It hits you like a ton of bricks—you recognize that prophecy is unfolding, but you're reluctant to voice your opinion.

God has a word for all of us!

But if you do warn the wicked person to turn from their ways and they do not do so, they will die for their sin, though you yourself will be saved. (Ezekiel 33:9)

They will *die*?! Wow! This is how much importance God places on the obligation of His people to watch. If we don't warn people, their blood will be on our hands.

When I [God] say to a wicked person, "You will surely die," and you do not warn them or speak out to dissuade them from their evil ways in order to save their life, that wicked person will die for their sin, and I will hold you accountable for their blood. (Ezekiel 3:18)

God told Ezekiel that his job was to warn the wicked. Please understand that the wicked aren't only the godless, but are also the apostate religious system, and if they don't turn from their ways, they will die in their sins.

In these last days, God has given each of us a spirit of Ezekiel, in that we can detect false prophets, counterfeit worship, and outright heresy, according to Matthew 24; however, if we don't watch and warn the people, see what God says:

> But if the watchman sees the sword coming and does not blow the trumpet to warn the people and the sword comes and takes someone's life, that person's life will be taken because of their sin, but I will hold the watchman accountable for their blood. (Ezekiel 33:6)

We as watchmen must sound the horn of the coming spiritual tsunami. Otherwise, we will be judged! Their blood will be on our hands. Our soul is at risk!

"But you're so negative!" I often hear this remark, especially from those who are involved in the modern-day religious system. It's interesting how the TV spotlight is on healing, casting out devils, and even prophecy, but the watchman are forced to take the back seat in the congregation. Few want to watch or even hear from those who are watching. Jesus encountered the same issue with His disciples immediately before He was apprehended to be crucified:

> Then he returned to his disciples and found them sleeping. "Couldn't you men keep watch with me for one hour?" he asked Peter. (Matthew 26:40)

Why was it necessary for Christ's closest, most intimate relationships to watch with Him? Because He knew what was to come, and so did His disciples; He had told them earlier what was going to happen. Many of God's people are reading Scripture and praying, but they're not watching! They might be sleeping or even equipping themselves for battle, but with blinders on. If we don't watch, then all the knowledge and prayers in the world won't deliver us if we don't see what the enemy is up to.

Within our *Last Evangelist* ministry, God has given us many warriors who pray and watch. Jesus left us with His authority and instructions for our work, but that doesn't mean people will listen. The prophet Jeremiah encountered that same issue:

> I appointed watchmen over you and said, "Listen to the sound of the trumpet!" But you said, "We will not listen." (Jeremiah 6:17)

Jeremiah didn't sign up to be God's watch warrior; he was *assigned* to the position. Notice that when it came to telling Israel what they *really* needed to hear, they didn't want to listen, and Jeremiah became very unpopular among his people.

Perhaps God has been speaking to you about your duty as a watchman. Don't ask if that's your job; you know by now that it is. Instead, consider asking God, "Lord, please keep me awake and alert." All the Father's children are connected to the window of what is now and what is to come.

In Matthew 24, Jesus' disciples asked Him to tell them when certain events would happen: "What will be the sign of your coming and of the end of the age?" (Matthew 24:3). Christ didn't answer their question; instead, He unveiled a list of things to watch for and gave two significant commands. First, "Watch out that no one deceives you" (Matthew 24:4), and second, "Keep watch" (Matthew 24:42).

Herein lies the reason God's people are weak and are knocked around by Satan's wicked culture! God's people aren't watching. If they were, then most preachers would be fired for sleeping on the job and replaced by one who is awake. Apostate church buildings would be closed down, and those demons would have to go elsewhere. When a preacher fails to speak the whole truth, the flock loses its 20/20 vision to spiritually watch. Why? Because they don't know what to *watch* for. Jesus says, "Watch that no one deceives you." Most preachers don't give spiritual eye examinations to their congregations because either they're being deceived or are leading others into deception! Hard words, huh? Thanks for the compliment. I'm right where God wants me to be: watching and warning!

So what did Jesus mean when He said, "Keep watch" in Matthew 24:42? Just that. We need to continually stay on high alert and not fall asleep spiritually. The demons know this is the final hour, and their time is short. God always warns us of what's to come. He promised He would never leave us, and He's right here with us now, with persuasive words of truth and warning.

You might be saying, "But I fast, I pray, and I read Scripture; however, I can't seem to get the victory that I know God wants for me." Try watching! I believe that one key element in a believer's life is to watch, and failing to watch is a way Satan gets to us through our flesh:

Watch and pray so that you will not fall into temptation. The spirit is willing, but the flesh is weak. (Mark 14:38)

Here, our Lord gives us truth about watching and praying. We must do both. Watching without communicating with God is as useless as praying without watching. God's people must start watching, remaining awake and aware of the times, the evil, and the coming days. Almost any professing Christian will tell you that Christ is returning; however, that's often the extent of their knowledge of that matter! They've given it no further thought, no investigation, or preparations.

Going from Watching to Warning

Son of man, I have made you a watchman for the people of Israel; so hear the word I speak and give them warning from me. (Ezekiel 33:7)

Throughout history, God has appointed watchmen, and reading the books of Isaiah, Jeremiah, and Ezekiel helps us understand the watchman's duty: to warn! It's vital to notice that God tells Ezekiel that *He, God,* will put *His* words in Ezekiel's mouth. When we start warning, then we must depend exclusively on the Holy Spirit to guide our words.

In order to warn and effectively announce to God's people what is happening, we must be equipped not with just spiritual truth, but with mental, emotional, and physical truth as well. We need mental truth, because we have the mind of Christ, and every thought enters through the mind. We need emotional truth, because thoughts affect our emotions and infiltrate the soul. Perhaps this is why so many people suffer from addictions, medicate themselves, or participate in New Age practices and self-help programs. We need physical truth, because God expects us to be equipped so we can continue to spread the Gospel and promote His kingdom. If we're not physically prepared, we are handicapped.

> Look, I come like a thief! Blessed is the one who stays awake and remains clothed, so as not to go naked and be shamefully exposed. (Revelation 16:15)

So, with our newly discovered commission, let us move forward with power, love, and a sound mind, being blessed as watch warriors until the end.

27

The Power of Persecution

In the world you will have tribulation.
But take heart; I have overcome the world.
JOHN 16:33

Because we are in perilous times and the Antichrist is quickly arising, perhaps this is the most pertinent chapter in this book. The emergence of the 2020 COVID-19 pandemic and mRNA vaccine has added fuel for persecution by enabling governments to infringe on Christians' rights to gather for worship while making exceptions for protests about media-hyped racial issues—protests that become violent, destructive riots. Scripture has already told us what will happen in these last days. Satan has used the pandemic and vaccine to bring tribulation, and tribulation brings persecution. God's Word is full of stories of godly people who were persecuted—even to death—just as our Lord was persecuted to death. He did not mince His words: "You will be handed over to the local councils and be flogged in the synagogues" (Matthew 10:17). In other words, we can expect to be treated as He was—for His name's sake. Right now, all over the world, Christians—true believers—are being persecuted and even beheaded for their faith.

Persecution presents itself much differently in Western culture than in other areas of the world. The worst persecution that an individual might suffer in the United States used to be ridicule, alienation, or losing a job for talking about Jesus in the workplace. In more extreme cases, it might escalate to a physical altercation. The 2020 pandemic opened the door for governments to order when, where, and even how Christians may worship, and the vaccine is dividing us even more. With the coronavirus shutdown, the "when" depended on when the pandemic was deemed to be over. The coronavirus prompted the government to implement restrictions whenever they felt it was "necessary." The "where" forced us to worship only at home while restrictions were in place. The "how" limited worship in small groups, whether groups were allowed at all, and social distancing requirements dictated that participants remain six feet apart. The vaccine has devastating side effects. As governments attempt to pass laws that mandate the vaccine, Christians will be forced to make hard choices, because without vaccine certification, it may be difficult to travel, or even to buy and sell.

Ultimately, the severity of persecution will increase for the true, remnant believers who choose to cling to Christ in the world's declining moral state. The 2020 outbreak was only the beginning of organized persecution against the Church in Western culture. The virus gave the government and society a foothold to dictate the regular activity of the church. Even while I was writing this book, persecution and civil unrest worsened considerably in the United States as well as globally. As Christians, we must be prepared and consider the words of Christ, "Be not deceived." We will either follow the counterfeit, one-world religious system or Christ's teaching. Even though we are "more than conquerors," great persecution will follow us as it did Jesus.

So, how can there be power in persecution? Persecution singles out people not merely because of their belief in Christianity but because they follow the ways of Christ. In other words, individuals are persecuted for their righteousness and how they actually follow Christ, not for simply identifying as Christian and going to church on Sundays.

> Blessed are you when people insult you, persecute you and falsely say all kinds of evil against you because of me. Rejoice and be glad, because great is your reward in heaven, for in the same way they persecuted the prophets who were before you. (Matthew 5:11–12)

The crucial part of Jesus' message is the phrase "for my name's sake." When true believers are really following Jesus, they're doing it for His name's sake. The problem with the modern-day church is that so-called Christians create their own god for their *own* sake. Jesus says that when we are true followers of Him and His ways, we will be persecuted by those who hate Him; *they* will hate us because we are doing what we do for God's name, and that's called "righteousness."

> He refreshes my soul. He guides me along the right paths for his name's sake. (Psalm 23:3)

In many families, especially years ago, namesakes were very important. Men and women wanted to uphold their family's name and not get involved with character traits or activities considered immoral, unethical, or illegal. Children who did engage in such immoral or unethical behaviors were typically cast out because their actions weren't aligned with the family's namesake. On the other hand, when children would uphold the family's name and operate within the guidelines of moral and ethical behavior, they were elevated to a high position in the family to the point of attaining power; this is what happens when children of God are persecuted in Jesus' name. They're automatically elevated in God's kingdom and are given even more power; the more persecution, the more power.

He gives strength to the weary and increases the power of the
weak. (Isaiah 40:29)

There is one condition for a child of God to receive this power and
use it, and that is the filling of the Holy Spirit. Yes, a believer must be
Spirit-filled. To understand the filling of the Spirit, if you haven't already,
please read chapter 15, "The Power of Repentance."

The Spirit-led believer is equipped with everything necessary to follow
Christ, pursue righteousness, and endure persecution for Jesus' name. God
grants His children the power to walk in obedience and face the perils of living *in* a fallen world while not being *of* the world. While God gives power
to the weak, the enemy attacks believers with a tactic we know as fear.

For the Spirit God gave us does not make us timid, but gives us
power, love and self-discipline. (2 Timothy 1:7)

From the very beginning, God knew that when we stand up for His
namesake, Satan attacks us with fear. God provides believers with the
power to follow Him fearlessly. Following God yields persecution, but
that's an indicator of righteousness and devotion to Christ. That's why
Jesus tells us to be glad when we're mistreated:

Rejoice and be glad, because great is your reward in heaven, for
in the same way they persecuted the prophets who were before
you. (Matthew 5:12)

God gives us the power to follow Him with love and a sound mind.
Following Him brings persecution, but persecution increases our power.
Therefore, as Matthew 5:12 proclaims, we need to rejoice because "great
is our reward" when we reach our heavenly home. That road home,
though, doesn't come without trials, tribulation, and even bribery. Here's
an example from our Lord's life:

Again, the devil took him to a very high mountain and showed him all the kingdoms of the world and their splendor. "All this I will give you," he said, "if you will bow down and worship me." (Matthew 4:8–9)

One could say that bribery is another of the enemy's tactics to steer us away from righteousness, but the closer we get to God's Spirit, the less important our flesh is! Denying the flesh and dying to self gives us immovable, unshakable power in Christ, and the enemy knows it, so he is continually trying to negotiate a better deal.

"You can have this lifestyle, or great wealth, or even fame, but there is a trade—your soul." This deal isn't offered blatantly or all at once—such as when Satan offered it to our Lord in the desert, and when the Antichrist offers the ultimate and final contract, the mark of the Beast. More than ever, the road is now paved for the Beast system to usher in a one-world government and religious system that will implement the final blow. *That* is the ultimate choice and the *road of no return.*

The purpose of this book is not to detail when, how, or what the mark specifically is, but to equip the believer to withstand that dark power. If Satan can slowly spoon-feed souls into cooperating with him (which he has), then here's the death clause in the contract:

It also forced all people, great and small, rich and poor, free and slave, to receive a mark on their right hands or on their foreheads, so that they could not buy or sell unless they had the mark, which is the name of the beast or the number of its name. (Revelation 13:16–17)

Believers will indeed have a difficult time surviving during this period, but remember that we are God's people, and He will *never leave us*! Greater is the *power in us* than the power in the evil one. (1 John 4:4: "You, dear children, are from God and have overcome them, because the one who is in you is greater than the one who is in the world.") Unfortunately, many will sign this contract with the father of hell, either by deception or desperation, but the outcome is the same: eternal damnation!

Once this deal is made, it's over. This contract cannot be canceled or made void:

A third angel followed them and said in a loud voice: "If anyone worships the beast and its image and receives its mark on their forehead or on their hand, they, too, will drink the wine of God's fury, which has been poured full strength into the cup of his wrath. They will be tormented with burning sulfur in the presence of the holy angels and of the Lamb. And the smoke of their torment will rise for ever and ever. There will be no rest day or night for those who worship the beast and its image, or for anyone who receives the Mark of its name." (Revelation 14:9–11)

Jesus told His disciples what would happen before He comes:

But before all this, they will seize you and persecute you. They will hand you over to synagogues and put you in prison, and you will be brought before kings and governors, and all on account of my name. (Luke 21:12)

Imprisonment May Be Persecution, but Slavery Is Not!

While it's true that the enemy can imprison a believer, it's important to remember that we, as true followers of Christ, are held prisoner (or slave) to only one thing: Christ and His Gospel. Right now, many brothers and sisters outside of America are being imprisoned because of their beliefs; however, it's safe to say that many are not slaves to the enemy of truth, because their true allegiance is to the Father alone. Paul was expressing that here in Philemon:

> Paul, a prisoner of Christ Jesus…
>   Paul—an old man and now also a prisoner of Christ Jesus. (Philemon 1:1, 9)

> No one can serve two masters. Either you will hate the one and love the other, or you will be devoted to the one and despise the other. You cannot serve both God and money. (Matthew 6:24)

The mark of the Beast will guarantee financial provision; at that point, we choose our master. We must choose Christ and Christ alone.

I need to convey how important it is for the believer to remember that persecution elevates us. This is the way we are designed by God. From the beginning, our Father knew that His children would walk through this "valley of the shadow of death." He makes sure that the winds of evil persecution actually become the very force under our wings, lifting us closer and closer to heaven. What the enemy intends for evil, God uses for good.

The Apostle Stephen was speaking truth to the religious crowd, so they stoned him to death. As he was dying, his spirit began to have 20/20 eternal vision. He actually witnessed heaven opening up and Christ standing at the Father's right hand side.

> When the members of the Sanhedrin heard this, they were furious and gnashed their teeth at him. But Stephen, full of the Holy Spirit, looked up to heaven and saw the glory of God, and Jesus standing at the right hand of God. "Look," he said, "I see heaven open and the Son of Man standing at the right hand of God." (Acts 7:54–56)

Stephen experienced this elevation of persecution as he was being stoned by the crowd, and he was being lifted up higher and higher. We should all yearn to see what Stephen saw. Some of us will, but only as the winds of hell come against God's people, so remember what our Lord said:

Blessed are those who are persecuted because of righteousness,
for theirs is the kingdom of heaven. (Matthew 5:10)

The kingdom of heaven belongs to us? Yes. Please understand that as a citizen of heaven, you are blessed and in good company, especially when you are persecuted! The next time you experience persecution, relax, feel God's power, and thank Him for the elevation.

That's how to benefit from the power of persecution.

28

The Power of God's 5G

It seems like every time I turn around, someone is talking about 5G and how evil and devastating it is. Some even claim that it's the primary weapon of the Antichrist. Some believe it has been used to create and spread the coronavirus pandemic. Simply put, 5G stands for fifth generation, which represents the level of cellular network technology. God has technology also; as a matter of fact, He has His own 5G network.

God's 5Gs are five valuable points in a believer's life that I consider "make it or break it" factors of being an influential Christian. These points give believers the ability to use and grow the God-given power they have within.

The First "G": Go to God

I don't mean go to church, to Bible study, or to prayer. I mean go to *God.* This kind of going to God is not an ordinary approach to our Father, but is a real visit to our Lord, sitting at the foot of His throne and understanding that He is God and is our only Source. This kind of "going to

God" doesn't involve anyone except ourselves and God, as there is no church, Bible study, or prayer partner that can go with us.

The Second "G": Get on Our Knees

How many of us go to God and yet never get on our knees? We may never humble ourselves or really bow to the presence of an omnipotent God. In fact, we may seem to have lost our fear of God, replacing it with the hyper-grace philosophy. This New-Age approach has managed to distort the fact that God is to be respected and honored and is not merely a "best friend." The truth is, God is an all-powerful force with the ability not only to destroy the body but to send the soul into hell for eternity.

The Third "G": Grant God Our Whole Life

In a last will and testament, grantors *give ownership of* everything they own (or a portion thereof) to beneficiaries. Most importantly, this is a *permanent* award to the beneficiaries; ownership cannot be taken back. Granting, however, is only the first step. Just as grantors give the beneficiaries ownership of all their material possessions, we, as God's children, grant our heavenly Father all we are and can become; we give Him ourselves.

The Fourth "G": Give God Everything We Have

It's one thing to grant God our lives; it's another to actually give Him our *possessions*. I remember a friend who bought his first house and was very excited about closing the sale and moving in. Several weeks later, he wasn't as cheerful. When I asked how he liked his new home, he told me that the closing had gone fine, and he officially owned the home, but the seller had never given him the keys. Not until the former owner relinquished the keys could my friend actually take possession of his new home. Do we treat our relationship with God the same way? Remember, when we go to God with a heart of humble repentance, it's then that we understand that all we have is legally His, and we don't own it anymore. But have we actually granted God everything? Or do we pick and choose what we will relinquish our rights to and what we'll keep? God owns everything, and requires us to grant Him everything. It's a sin to keep what isn't ours. We give God our worries, our anxiety, our passions, our careers, our relationships, our finances…everything.

The Fifth "G": Grow

Growing in God is only possible through the steps listed above. So-called Christians try to appear mature with microwave techniques such as acquiring a ministry degree for the status of credentials, attending church for show, performing "religious" activities, and even engaging their creative talents to masquerade their ego. True growth is only gained through the testing of our faith, which produces perseverance and maturity.

> Consider it pure joy, my brothers and sisters, whenever you face trials of many kinds, because you know that the testing of your faith produces perseverance. Let perseverance finish its work so that you may be mature and complete, not lacking anything. (James 1:2–4)

Only through real growth in God can we actually receive supernatural joy through trials and tribulations.

After a Christian has reached 5G, then it is always important to return to 1G and start over again; this process will cease only when we take our last breath or when Christ returns.

> Therefore, I urge you, brothers and sisters, in view of God's mercy, to offer your bodies as a living sacrifice, holy and pleasing to God—this is your true and proper worship. Do not conform to the pattern of this world, but be transformed by the renewing of your mind. Then you will be able to test and approve what God's will is—his good, pleasing and perfect will. (Romans 12:1–2)

This Scripture passage sums up the essence of this chapter. By following these five simple steps, the 5Gs, we resist conforming to this world. Then our minds transform so that we can think and perform like Christ. Because we have the mind of our Lord, we will know His good, pleasing, and perfect will. The next time someone wants to discuss 5G, don't forget to tell them about *God's 5Gs*.

29

The Power of Prayer

First of all, prayer is not *power*. Prayer is communication with God. However, when we put our God-given power into action (the power that comes from communicating with God in spirit and truth), amazing things happen.

Communication with God should always be effective, but no prayer can be effective on its own. The effective part of prayer comes from the individual. We must be righteous before God. James 5:16 says:

> Confess your trespasses to one another, and pray for one another that you may be healed. The effective, fervent prayer of a righteous man avails much.

A righteous man? Does this mean we need to be walking on water? Holier than thou? No, righteousness means walking with God, depending on Him, believing that *He is*, knowing that He does what he says He will do, and recognizing that "He is a rewarder of those who diligently seek Him" (Hebrews 11:6). We are righteous in Jesus Christ when we know that *He* is our Savior, and we earnestly seek Him daily.

The following examples show the differences between a power*ful* and a power*less* prayer:

Laura is single and has been dating Jim for several months, so she goes to the Lord:

Lord, I've been asking you for a mate, someone I can marry. I'm asking now regarding Jim. He seems so nice, and I'd like to know if I should continue to date him. Would you please give me an answer? A sign? A direction? In Jesus' Name, Amen.

The Lord instructs Laura to fast for three days, including fasting from Jim (not seeing him). Before her three-day fast, Laura informs Jim that she needs a few days apart to sort through some things.

On the third day, Laura sees Jim having dinner with another woman. He's drinking wine (which she has never known him to do), appears to be having a good time, and seems very friendly toward this woman.

After her fast, Laura goes on a date with Jim. She asks him what he's been doing for the past three days. Jim tenderly tells her that he's really been missing her. When she confronts him about seeing him with the other woman and drinking wine, he tells her that the other woman is *only a friend*, and that he was drinking because he was so *sad*, missing Laura.

Laura is shocked at his answer. What does she do with this situation? She has three choices:

Choice 1: Laura does not go back to God at all.

Choice 2: Laura tells God that it all turned out so horribly, and maybe she should not have been away from Jim for three days, because it obviously upset him and caused him to be overly friendly with another woman, and even caused him to drink alcohol. She also says to God that maybe it should have been only a one-day fast.

Maybe, Lord, it was Satan who moved in, trying to destroy my relationship with Jim. Oh Lord, I'm so confused as to what's going on, it's a mess. Help me; I need an answer.

Choice 3: Laura prays:

Father God, I came to you with my dilemma. I laid it out before your throne, believing I would receive the answer from you. Based on what I know in your Holy Word, I believe this is my answer. I will not date Jim anymore, and I truly believe you have the right man for me in the future if it is your will for me to have a husband. I thank you, and I pray in Jesus' Name, Amen.

Which response would please the Father?

If any of you lacks wisdom, you should ask God, who gives generously to all without finding fault, and it will be given to you. But when you ask, you must believe and not doubt, because the one who doubts is like a wave of the sea, blown and tossed by the wind. That person should not expect to receive anything from the Lord. Such a person is double-minded and unstable in all they do. (James 1:5–8)

In the third response, Laura is not double-minded; she believes God's Word, acts on it, and moves on.

Once God gives us an answer, we should never look back or contemplate the past as a mistake. Jesus said in Matthew 8:22:

Follow Me, and let the dead bury their own dead.

Life is constantly changing with continual movement. God is a God of motion, movement, and future; He is always moving forward toward His ultimate plan.

If the definition of insanity is doing the same thing over and over again, expecting different results, here's the definition of the prayer of insanity: Praying for the same thing over and over again but never believing God can or will answer, or not accepting the answer He gives. Too many Christians have turned into a pillar of salt. They're frozen in their past mistakes and failures. They asked but did not believe, so they keep asking but never believing.

> Therefore I tell you, whatever you ask for in prayer, believe that you have received it, and it will be yours. (Mark 11:24)

Imagine Laura continuing to go to the Father and petitioning Him about her problem, then coming back to God yet again, making every excuse in the world for the outcome, except for the fact that God *did* answer her prayer. It was quite unmistakable. He did deal with her petition.

It doesn't matter if we're praying for deliverance, wisdom, provision, or anything else; the principle is the same. We must come as children expecting God to be there for us. It is impossible to please God without faith.

That's the power of praying with a single mind.

30

The Power of Transfiguration

After six days Jesus took with him Peter, James and John the brother of James, and led them up a high mountain by themselves. There he was transfigured before them. His face shone like the sun, and his clothes became as white as the light. Just then there appeared before them Moses and Elijah, talking with Jesus.

MATTHEW 17:1–3

Obviously, it was important to God for the disciples to witness Christ actually changing bodily form. There are many studies on reasons it was crucial for them to see this, including so that they could see God's power and to teach us not to build altars, especially to a man.

Peter said to Jesus, "Lord, it is good for us to be here. If you wish, I will put up three shelters—one for you, one for Moses and one for Elijah." While he was still speaking, a bright cloud covered them, and a voice from the cloud said, "This is my Son, whom I love; with him I am well pleased. Listen to him." (Matthew 17:4–5)

The disciples wanted to erect monuments to Jesus, Moses, and Elijah. God informed them that Christ was the focus; He was the Father's most-loved Son, in whom God is well pleased. This is sometimes the core message of most preachers, and while this teaching is correct, I'd like to present another possibility as to why God allowed us to have this information.

> Do not conform to the pattern of this world, but be transformed by the renewing of your mind. Then you will be able to test and approve what God's will is—his good, pleasing and perfect will. (Romans 12:2)

What does this have to do with being transfigured?

When the mind is renewed into the mind of Christ, something happens that's referred to as "transformation." Many scholars immediately call this "transformation" a "transfiguration," but there is a difference between the two terms. Transfiguration is a significant change in appearance, shape, or form; transformation is the act of transforming or changing, or the state of being transformed.

Though these words are similar, what separates them is the degree of change. Some would argue that God never intends for us to take a different shape or form; however, Philippians 3:20–21 says otherwise:

> But our citizenship is in heaven. And we eagerly await a Savior from there, the Lord Jesus Christ, who, by the power that enables him to bring everything under his control, will transform our lowly bodies so that they will be like his glorious body.

I would definitely call this "transfiguration," and even though it will happen when Christ returns, I believe the change starts here on earth with each believer the minute he or she repents and follows Christ.

That's a bold statement, huh? When we, as God's children, operate in the anointing, truly follow our purpose, and use the mind of Christ, something begins to happen. First, there is an actual change in our thinking; then, our behavior changes. Finally, there is an ultimate difference in our being. Because we have the mind of Christ, when we start imitating Him, it's only logical that we would be more like Him. Now, most of us would assume that this could only mean we would be more like Him spiritually. If, however, we are complete in our purpose and behaving like Jesus, then our bodies will enjoy the benefit of such a great spiritual, emotional, and mental state of existence. I've actually seen believers physically morph from being weak, pale, sickly, and insecure into vibrant, healthy, bold warriors of God. God willing, we should all expect to be strong, disease-free, and have full-power confidence. This might involve eating a healthier diet, getting more exercise, having better posture, and engaging in a deeper prayer life with thanksgiving and praise to strengthen our faith. Remember what Jesus said to the woman who touched His robe and was healed instantly from the issue of blood? Jesus said her faith had made her whole. Her blood underwent a complete transfiguration, from weak and sick to perfect. When we accept Christ into our lives and live for God, we experience a transfiguration from being an eternally lost soul to becoming a child of the Living God, full of power, love, and a sound mind.

Now that's the power of transfiguration.

31

The Power of True Worship

How would we respond if we walked into church for service to find that the form of worship had been *changed*? Instead of standing in a sanctuary with the congregation, raising our hands, opening hymnals, and singing with a band or choir, what if we were ushered into our own private booth to worship as the Spirit leads? If we were alone, and even without music, only the sweet music of the Holy Spirit, how different would our worship be? Would we even be able to worship at all? Would we find it difficult to give God everything we have in the form of praise, knowing that is what He really wants?

Mark 14:3–9 gives us an example of true worship:

While he was in Bethany, reclining at the table in the home of Simon the Leper, a woman came with an alabaster jar of very expensive perfume, made of pure nard. She broke the jar and poured the perfume on his head.

Some of those present were saying indignantly to one another, "Why this waste of perfume? It could have been sold for more than a year's wages and the money given to the poor." And they rebuked her harshly.

"Leave her alone," said Jesus. "Why are you bothering her?

She has done a beautiful thing to me. The poor you will always have with you, and you can help them any time you want. But you will not always have me. She did what she could. She poured perfume on my body beforehand to prepare for my burial. Truly I tell you, wherever the gospel is preached throughout the world, what she has done will also be told, in memory of her."

This woman was on a mission, a premeditated, thoroughly planned out, and detailed mission to be in a place of true worship. She apparently was given spiritual wisdom that no one else either possessed or was aware of. This is what she knew:

1. Jesus was a king. (He had just ridden through town on a donkey while having palm leaves waved at Him, in fulfillment of Old Testament prophecy.)
2. A king deserves to be honored.
3. He would die. The woman poured out the perfume as a symbol of Christ's death for His body to be anointed.
4. She gave the very best perfume that she had, and she gave Him all of it.
5. She was silent. She spoke no words explaining to anyone what she was doing. She didn't ask for anyone's advice. She didn't solicit a "praise report."
6. She was a doer. She didn't tell anyone what she was doing ahead of time. She didn't even desire an audience, save for her *King*.

Those who witnessed what the woman did and then rebuked her show us that, as true worshipers, we might be ridiculed (even by Christians) because what we're doing may not be the way they would have done it. It might seem illogical to them, whether they think we're spending too much money or wasting our time. This woman didn't care about any of that, because she was simply *focused on her King*.

After she was ridiculed, Jesus defended her. When we worship in spirit and in truth, Christ will always be there to protect us from the arrows of discouragement and criticism. Basically, Jesus put everyone in their place by telling them that Mary was doing the right and blessed thing.

When we worship in spirit and truth, you can bet it will be seen by many, both by the saved and unsaved. This week, will you be another follower of Jesus Christ, standing in church doing the same thing everyone else is doing? Or will you have the power to be a true worshiper of Almighty God? This doesn't mean we want to draw attention to ourselves, but when we are focused on the Lord in spirit and truth, authentic worship is inevitable.

God says our worship will be memorialized when we are led by the Holy Spirit. In other words, "true worship" will be remembered by generations to come. That's the power of true worship.

The Power in the Blood

Most of us sing hymns such as "Power in the Blood," "Nothing but the Blood of Jesus," and "Are You Washed in the Blood?". I call these the "blood songs." Even though we may have sung them hundreds of times, have we really listened to the words and digested the true meaning of the "blood of Christ"? Our eternal outcome, our lifeblood, and our very existence depend on the blood of Jesus. Without the spilling of His blood, *nothing* is possible; *nothing* would exist. Life is in the blood.

Four Stages of Blood

The blood of our precious Savior was pivotal at four different points in God's overall plan for the salvation of humanity

The Blood Entered the World as a Baby

The first time God's blood was introduced into the world was when Jesus was a baby. Unfortunately, the pagan church and its tradition have turned that event into an annual celebration of a defenseless child lying in a manger. On the contrary, the same power that ran through the veins of Jesus as an adult was the same blood (with the same power) in the Christ-child, and this blood held the power to cast out demons and resurrect the dead.

The Blood Flowed through Christ

Because God's blood was in His Son, Christ was able to carry out the Father's perfect will, which is summed up in Jesus' birth, life, death, and resurrection, which was only possible through and by the blood. His blood stood against the legion of demons and cast them into the herd of swine. His blood healed the centurion soldier's servant by merely speaking the word. His word fed thousands with only a few pieces of fish.

The Blood Spilled at Christ's Crucifixion

It was *not* the *suffering* of God's Son that gives us eternal life, it was the spilling of His blood to the point of death. When Christ died on the cross, He spoke three words that changed everything: "It is finished" (John 19:39).

The Blood Defeated Death in the Resurrection

The resurrection is the ultimate display of God's power, in that it broke the chains of hell, defeated death, and provided salvation for God's chosen. Jesus actually rose to the Father and offered His own blood as a substitute for our blood. Understand that the power that brought Christ to life and took Him to the Father's throne was the very same power in baby Jesus' blood, the same power enabling Christ's miracles, and the same power you and I possess.

If you and I possess the same power as Christ had, and His power is in His blood, then my question is, "Is the blood of Christ alive today?"

Does the Blood of Christ Flow Today?

But when Christ came as high priest of the good things that are now already here, he went through the greater and more perfect tabernacle that is not made with human hands, that is to say, is not a part of this creation. He did not enter by means of the blood of goats and calves; but he entered the Most Holy Place once for all by his own blood, thus obtaining eternal redemption. The blood of goats and bulls and the ashes of a heifer sprinkled on those who are ceremonially unclean sanctify them so that they are outwardly clean. How much more, then, will the blood of Christ, who through the eternal Spirit offered himself unblemished to God, cleanse our consciences from acts that lead to death, so that we may serve the living God. (Hebrews 9:11–14)

The blood of goats offered in the ancient Jewish system of sacrifice was temporary; that's why the priests had to offer it repeatedly. It wasn't ever-flowing blood. When Christ offered His blood to the Father, however, it was alive then, and today, it is just as alive! Otherwise, another lamb would have to be sacrificed. Christ Jesus is the Eternal Lamb.

You'd be surprised at the number of Christians and even pastors who agree that Christ's birth, life, death, and resurrection are confirmed historical events. But if Christ is the same yesterday, today, and tomorrow, and has always existed, isn't His blood still as alive today as it was yesterday?

But if we walk in the light, as he is in the light, we have fellowship with one another, *and the blood of Jesus, his Son, purifies us from all sin.* (1 John 1:7, emphasis added)

Notice the verse says that the blood of Jesus purifies us of *all* sin. This statement is in the present tense; it cleanses us now. It isn't only retroactive or past tense, it's in the *now*. Yes, the blood is as active today as it has always been! That's why Christ could transfer His authority to His disciples. *We* are now the recipients of this incredible power!

> They triumphed over him by the blood of the Lamb and by the word of their testimony; they did not love their lives so much as to shrink from death. (Revelation 12:11)

Christians often quote the words from Scripture, "We are more than conquerors." However, what are we conquerors of? We're more than conquerors of Satan. While it's true that we are victors over the evil one, it's only by the blood of the Lamb and the word of our testimony. What's our testimony? Christ. What does Christ possess? The blood.

What does the blood do? It heals, conquers, and saves by cleansing us from all sin. But there's one other amazing thing the blood of Christ does. It *protects*. The most exceptional example of the blood's protection was when God passed through Egypt, killing the Egyptians' firstborn.

> On that same night I will pass through Egypt and strike down every firstborn of both people and animals, and I will bring judgment on all the gods of Egypt. I am the LORD. (Exodus 12:12)

Notice that God said He would take out "every" firstborn. "Every" includes even the firstborn of the Israelites. God offered His chosen people an exemption clause, though: He instructed the Israelites to sprinkle the blood of a lamb over their door frame.

> Then they are to take some of the blood and put it on the sides and tops of the doorframes of the houses where they eat the lambs. (Exodus 12:7)

God told them that He would pass over the homes where He saw the blood on the doorframe.

> When the LORD goes through the land to strike down the Egyptians, he will see the blood on the top and sides of the doorframe and will pass over that doorway, and he will not permit the destroyer to enter your houses and strike you down. (Exodus 12:23)

To me, this is a preview of how Jesus' blood actually protects us today. How does the blood protect us?

> The seventy-two returned with joy, saying, "Lord, even the demons are subject to us in your name." (Luke 10:17)

Of course, we can't cast out demons without God's protection, and these seventy-two knew that. They were amazed that at the sound of Jesus' name, the demons submitted. Without the protection of Jesus' blood, however, no demon will submit.

Apply the Blood

What about the blood of Jesus? Can we use it today? If so, how do we apply it? Is it even applicable? When Jesus said, "Greater things you will do than I," does that have anything to do with His blood? Some TV "preachers" have hijacked the term "pleading the blood," turning it into a carnival sideshow. Should we allow Satan to distort what could be the pivotal point of victory? Scripture doesn't say, "The blood *did* cleanse us," it says, "it *does* cleanse us," so clearly it is a relevant and active force today. "Pleading" is a legal term, not an act of begging. Attorneys use it when stating the merits of their case. In countries that follow the English model of law, a pleading is a formal written statement of a party's claim or defense to another party's claim in a civil action. The *pleading* defines the issue to be adjudicated, the problem that requires a formal judgment or decision.

Though we're not on trial or in a physical courtroom, we can still present the fact that we stand on the blood of Christ, meaning that our foundation is the life, death, and resurrection of the precious blood of the Lamb. For me, the following Scripture sums up what I need to know.

> I pray that the eyes of your heart may be enlightened in order that you may know the hope to which he has called you, the riches of his glorious inheritance in his holy people, and his incomparably great power for us who believe. That power is the same as the mighty strength he exerted when he raised Christ from the dead and seated him at his right hand in the heavenly realms, far above all rule and authority, power and dominion, and every name that is invoked, not only in the present age but also in the one to come. And God placed all things under his feet and appointed him to be head over everything for the church, which is his body, the fullness of him who fills everything in every way. (Ephesians 1:18–23)

Verse 18 prays that "the eyes of my heart be opened." I can supernaturally see my true inheritance, everything my Father has given me, and what I will receive in the future.

Verses 19 and 20 tell me what I definitely have now: power, and lots of it. As a matter of fact, I have the same ability the Father used to raise Christ from the dead.

Verses 21–23 verify the level of the power I have received, including who and what this power rules over. We rule over everything—all things. This is why we need to understand that through the blood of our Savior,

God's eternal Lamb, we've not only inherited the same power that God possesses, we actually have it *now*...but only through the blood of Jesus. When we acknowledge it, we have the authority and rule "far above all rule and authority, power and dominion, and every name invoked, not only in the present age but also in the one to come."

That's the true power in the blood.

33

The Power of God's Calling

What if life plays out like a movie and, as each moment unfolds, the plot thickens? This movie will premiere only once; there will be no sequels, reruns, or remakes. There will be no way to rewind or redo any scene. As a filmmaker, I can tell you that a film always starts with a script. Then you need actors to play each character, and a crew to film it.

God's Script

God has written the greatest script ever, and then He sent His Son Jesus to produce it. The script is God's Word, which explains everything in life that deals with eternity. It's a drama, it's a comedy, it's rated G, and it's rated X! When Jesus came, it was the beginning of the production of what we could call the final scenes Christ spoke about in Matthew 24. He said that before He left, He would send the director, the Comforter, the one who would guide us through these final scenes: the Holy Spirit.

Our Role

We, as God's children, imitate God in many ways, primarily through our creativity. Filmmaking is an imitation of what God is doing. In this script (the Bible), the "actors" aren't people playing roles; they are created specifically for each character in God's wonderful epic. We must understand that when God wrote His script, He had you and I in mind for the very special roles we are to play. God tailor-made us uniquely for our particular character in His beautiful story of redemption.

> Before I formed you in the womb I knew you, before you were born I set you apart; I appointed you as a prophet to the nations. (Jeremiah 1:5)

Like Jeremiah, God knew us before we were formed in the womb; once we were born, He knew every hair on our head (Matthew 10:30). As God's chosen actor, have you committed to signing your contract with Him for life?

Only you can play your role. When I'm casting for a movie, I spend days auditioning numerous actors. Sometimes I audition even hundreds of actors to find that one person to play a specific role no one else can play. Have you ever seen a movie in which it was evident that an actor was definitely meant to play his or her role?

Once I select the actor, we sign the contract and begin filming. However, there are times the actor doesn't show up on set. Do they make up excuses? You bet! I've heard many explanations, such as "I forgot," "I was too busy," "I want more money," "I was afraid," or, "I got lost on the way to the set." When this happens, I'm forced to recast the role and replace the actor. Have you broken your contract with God?

Our Contract

Every true Christian has a signed contract with the Father. That contract is signed in blood by Christ on the cross; the intent is for it never to be broken. The question you and I must ask ourselves is this: Are we living the terms of the contract? The most important term of the contract is showing up on the set of the film. Have you done that? God has called many of His actors to the film set, but few show up: "For many are invited, but few are chosen" (Matthew 22:14). Has God been calling you? Have you made excuses about not showing up?

We all have excuses such as, "Oh God, I'm not good enough; haven't you seen my past? Don't you know who I really am?" or "Oh God, I'm busy right now, but tomorrow I will be there. Can you get someone else to play my part until then?"

> He [Jesus] said to another man, "Follow me." But he replied, "Lord, first let me go and bury my father." Jesus said to him, "Let the dead bury their own dead, but you go and proclaim the kingdom of God." Still another said, "I will follow you, Lord; but first let me go back and say goodbye to my family." Jesus replied, "No one who puts a hand to the plow and looks back is fit for service in the kingdom of God." (Luke 9:59–62)

Movie stars have stand-ins who are hired to substitute for the real actors while the camera crew sets up lighting and frames the shot. When everyone is ready to film the scene, the real actors step in. God, however, doesn't use stand-ins. He wants the real actors; He wants commitment.

Many scenes that I film require people to be "extras" or "atmosphere." They're in the background to perform actions like walking by or sitting in a restaurant. When a Christian doesn't show up to the set, I can imagine a situation where the director, the Holy Spirit, goes to the producer, Jesus, and says, "The actor didn't show up again; what do we do?" Then Jesus looks at a group of extras, points, and says, "Choose one of them to play the part!"

There is a point when God will no longer call someone:

Just as they [the "actors"] did not think it worthwhile to retain the knowledge of God, God gave them over to a depraved mind, so that they do what ought not to be done. (Romans 1:28)

Yet we wonder why the body of Christ is struggling today, and why Christians are weak and sick.

Are We Playing the Wrong Role?

Maybe we've shown up on the set, but things have never felt right. It's never really come together; it's always a struggle. Could it be that you or I are playing the wrong part? Are we trying to play someone else's role? Too many Christians today want to imitate other believers for various reasons. Maybe because these others are well-received, and their message is loved by many. Or maybe it's the way a certain church does things. Or maybe someone simply wants to fit in, so he or she just goes along with the program.

Imitating other believers is a deadly mistake for many reasons. The person or system we're following might be teaching a false gospel. If we are playing someone else's role, no one is playing the part we, the "chosen" actors, are cast to play. For example, while you may be busy feeding the homeless because it's what your church does, no one may be teaching that specific Bible study that's supposed to be taught—by you! Why? Because you, the "actor," are busy with some church program so you're not doing what you're supposed to be doing. In the film world, we call this "rewriting the script." When an actor doesn't play the assigned part, it's time to rewrite the script.

Memorize Our Lines

One of the most irritating traits of deadbeat actors is when they show up on the set and don't know their lines. Why do they fail? Because they haven't studied. They haven't spent time working on the script like they were contracted to do.

The Bible is God's script, and His words are our dialogue. When we spend time studying Scripture, the Holy Spirit guides us through it. He enables us to be the powerhouse Christians we are created to be. When we don't spend time with God studying His Word, we are forced to rewrite His script; it's like trying to push a square peg into a round hole.

Ok, so maybe we do have our lines memorized, and perhaps we're playing the correct part, but we're not hitting the mark. When we film a scene, we rehearse with each actor where and when he or she is supposed to move. We establish lighting so the actors will be visible at each position. The camera follows according to the lighting that's set during rehearsal. There are marks on the floor so the actor knows exactly where to be during the scene. When an actor doesn't hit the mark, many things happen, and they're not good. Here are a few things can happen when we don't hit the mark.

We Can Upstage and Block Other Actors

Are we upstaging our brothers and sisters in Christ? Some are trying to do what God has called them to do, but they lose the spotlight to someone who naturally has more talent or ability. God doesn't choose us for His service according to our talent alone; He chooses based on our anointing.

Way too many preachers are in the pulpit only because they are good speakers. Unfortunately, they may not be anointed. The same goes for some music leaders. Some actually have no business leading worship; they are not appointed to that ministry spiritually. Sure, they may have natural talent, but without the anointing, they are ineffective. Worse yet, they may be misleading the flock. Every actor in God's movie is chosen by God and is anointed because they are appointed by God.

We Can End up in the Shadows

Actors who don't hit their mark end up in the shadows because the lighting is specific; if we're not on our designated mark, then no one may see us. Is this you? I used to think that Christians hiding in the shadows were very righteous and that their behavior demonstrated a form of humility. However, this is a lie from hell. God has called us to get on stage and play that role with all our heart. Maybe we avoid the mark because we don't want to be discovered as a Christian because we're not living like one, or we're afraid of persecution.

We Can Delay the Entire Production

Actors who don't hit the mark slow everything down. What would typically take five minutes to shoot might instead require five hours. Everyone suffers, just like the whole Body of Christ does when well-meaning believers are not hitting their mark.

Every second that passes, a scene is being filmed in our Father's epic production. You and I are the stars. When we face the Author and Finisher of our faith on that day, will we hear "Well done, good and faithful servant" or "Depart from me, I never knew you"?

When we hear God's calling, we must commit to show up to the set with dialog memorized. When we hit our mark, it's at that point that we achieve the ultimate height of our anointing, which results in total victory and deliverance.

That's the power of God's calling on our life.

34

The Power of Exposing the Enemy

Why should true believers, when guided by the Holy Spirit, challenge the counterfeit church and oppose apostasy? Because the world interprets church buildings as God's house and church people as God's representatives. Therefore, it's vital to protect and honor God's character since the world judges God by the integrity of the church.

For example, imagine being pulled over by someone in a police uniform, but then you discover he really doesn't have a badge; he's trying to use an officer's authority. He is an impersonator. Would he go to jail?

Imagine hiring legal counsel, but later finding out that your "attorney" never went to law school and barely graduated high school. She's a fraud. Would she go to jail?

Imagine being operated on, but then learning the "surgeon" isn't a doctor at all, only someone who wants to make a lot of money and appear important. He is an imposter. Would he go to jail?

Anyone, though, can start a church and "represent the living God," spew lies, manipulate congregants' understanding of God's character, lead souls to hell, and apparently suffer no consequences (at least not in this lifetime).

To expose the enemy, we must first know who the enemy is. Next, we must understand his tactics and agenda. Throughout Scripture, God links evil with snakes. In Genesis, we read about the serpent, the very embodiment of evil, in the Garden of Eden. And when Jesus identified the religious hypocrites in His day, He called them "snakes" and a "brood of vipers" before saying, " How will you escape being condemned to hell?" (Matthew 23:33).

Why did Jesus refer to these religious leaders as a "brood of vipers," comparing the religious community to one of the deadliest types of snakes? Vipers sink long-hinged fangs into their victims and, in many countries, their bite is considered a death sentence. During Jesus' time, when farmers burned the brush off of their land to prepare for planting, they expected to encounter a brood of vipers. Often these vipers would scramble to escape the fire, but wouldn't make it; they would burn in the flames. When Jesus told the religious people that they would not escape hell's fire, it symbolized the vipers that were unable to escape a farmer's fire.

> Woe to you, teachers of the law and Pharisees, you hypocrites!
> You shut the door of the kingdom of heaven in people's faces.
> You yourselves do not enter, nor will you let those enter who are
> trying to. (Matthew 23:13)

Here Christ is saying the Pharisees had hijacked the truth of His Father's love, plan, and relationship with humanity, and instead had created a counterfeit interpretation and representation of God's character. Not only would they *not* inherit the kingdom of God, but they were also restricting others from entering righteousness.

The counterfeit church is like a viper: When it injects its deadly venom, the result is spiritual death—unless specific steps are immediately taken. In most churches today, we don't see much that represents the early church, which gathered secretly, hungering for the truth their

Messiah revealed. Instead, today, we see man-made denominations, traditions, and false teachings. Today's church looks more like Starbucks sponsoring a rock concert. Remember, the church today stems from the unified religion established by the Roman emperor, Constantine. He wanted more control, so he merged all religions into one. He forced Christians to worship on Sunday, a day that had been designated for worship of the sun god. Constantine also added practices such as Easter, Christmas, and Halloween, which still exist. The enemy who wanted to kill Jesus then is the same one who wants Him dead now. Even though Jesus isn't here physically, the enemy certainly doesn't want the Holy Spirit present. The question is, why does the enemy want to get rid of God?

> Jesus then began to speak to them in parables: "A man planted a vineyard. He put a wall around it, dug a pit for the winepress and built a watchtower. Then he rented the vineyard to some farmers and moved to another place. At harvest time he sent a servant to the tenants to collect from them some of the fruit of the vineyard. But they seized him, beat him and sent him away empty-handed. Then he sent another servant to them; they struck this man on the head and treated him shamefully. He sent still another, and that one they killed. He sent many others; some of them they beat, others they killed.
>
> "He had one left to send, a son, whom he loved. He sent him last of all, saying, 'They will respect my son.'
>
> "But the tenants said to one another, 'This is the heir. Come, let's kill him, and the inheritance will be ours.' So they took him and killed him, and threw him out of the vineyard." (Mark 12:1–8)

Jesus revealed that this religious system had a pattern of deafening the voice of prophets speaking truth. One truth was that the Pharisees and Sadducees created a false religion.

At the conclusion of this passage from Mark, our Lord delivered the final blow of truth as He unveiled the snakes' full intentions of killing Him. Finally, Christ disclosed their ultimate and quite simple reason for wanting to take Him out of the picture: The enemy wants the inheritance. The first thing Satan wants is what every true child of God possesses—power. Many Christians aren't using their God-given power, and many don't even know they own it. The second thing Satan is salivating over is the kingdom of God. The devil wants ultimate authority over it; the battle over heavenly treasures manifests in the flesh on earth as a counterfeit relationship with the True God. Like the cancer that devastates one's physical health, there's also spiritual cancer that devastates one's spiritual life. There are four stages of its progression:

1. Confusion
2. Compromise
3. Complacency
4. Contagiousness

Stage 1 Cancer: Confusion

Confusion is the main culprit and the beginning of this deadly disease. Many of us were either born into a family that was affiliated with a particular religious denomination or had religion waved under our noses by someone who (though well-meaning) gave us a bad taste when it came to God. To get to the truth, we have to first undo the confusion caused by all the lies of religion. Sometimes, it's not a matter of seeking out the truth of God; He is always with us, but His real love may be camouflaged, strategically covered up by the enemy. Therefore, we must first ask God to lead us into truth, light, and a right relationship with Him. Second, we need to read Scripture. Instead of starting with John 3:16, let's start with 2 Peter 2:1:

But there were also false prophets among the people, just as there will be false teachers among you. They will secretly introduce destructive heresies, even denying the sovereign Lord who bought them—bringing swift destruction on themselves.

Modern-day con artists are denying God by creating a false god that will allow the members of the congregation to do most anything they want under the rule of grace. This "Candyland Christ" is politically correct, never offensive, and is always seeker-friendly. Killing pre-born babies, excusing perversion, and embracing a New-Age worldview are often part of their doctrine.

Many follow their depraved conduct and bring the way of truth into disrepute. In their greed, these teachers will exploit their followers with fabricated stories. Their condemnation has long been hanging over them, and their destruction has not been sleeping.

For if God did not spare angels when they sinned, but sent them to hell, putting them in chains of darkness to be held for judgment. (2 Peter 2:2–4)

Scripture says we should expect that these lying, deceiving, false teachers are out to get our soul.

Stage 2 Cancer: Compromise

Of course, if we're confused about who God really is, then it's easier to compromise the truth. Every believer knows in his or her heart when he or she is doing something that goes against the guidelines of living in God's kingdom, but few respond to this small voice of warning. As we continue rejecting the little voice, it gradually fades. Hence, it becomes easier to compromise.

Stage 3 Cancer: Complacency

Complacency is more comfortable when compromise becomes a way of life. Scripture says that God turns people over to their sins after a certain period of warning. Once we move into this stage of complacency, it takes nothing short of a crisis to wake us; even then, it's difficult.

Stage 4 Cancer: Contagiousness

When spiritual cancer metastasizes, the carrier automatically passes it on to everyone else they come in contact with—and sometimes merely by default (when the victim doesn't possess truth). I've preached, led worship, and attended all kinds of churches (from congregations of only a few to those numbering in the thousands). If they're stricken with this religious venom, the symptoms are the same, though they may manifest in different ways. The poison in the seeker-friendly church is the most difficult to discern because the enemy uses *culture* to strike its victims. This church is no more than a movie theater, rock concert arena, or self-help seminar spewing Scripture out of context. As stated earlier, many of these churches have even welcomed New-Age philosophies. Practices include using marijuana to "better understand God" and using micro-breweries serving craft beers in an effort to "reach the lost." This type of church often is dominated by one family with a strong, cult-like hold on the direction of its false teaching and tactics.

No matter which false church you may be coming out of (or are still involved with), the result is always the same—eternal damnation. Wait a minute! Eternal damnation? That's pretty harsh and absolute. Let's look at the book of Revelation, where we read what Jesus says to one of the seven churches:

I know your deeds, that you are neither cold nor hot. I wish you were either one or the other! So, because you are lukewarm—neither hot nor cold—I am about to spit you out of my mouth. (Revelation 3:15–16)

"Lukewarm" doesn't mean a church is being solemn or sensational; it's a condition of spiritual truth. A lukewarm church can appear to be on fire for God, giving prophecy and healing people, but inside, its people are "dead man's bones." These are the churches to whom Jesus responds:

I don't know you or where you come from. Away from me, all you evildoers! (Luke 13:27).

Churches become lukewarm because of spiritual cancer, not because of how outwardly active their congregations are.

Now, what's the antidote to that viper venom?

What then will the owner of the vineyard do? He will come and kill those tenants and give the vineyard to others. (Mark 12:9)

It's not a matter of what *we* will do. It's a matter of what *God* will do.

God says He will take the vineyard from the husbandmen and give it to us, His chosen. Also, it's important for us to proclaim that God will destroy the counterfeit church, which is existing on borrowed time.

What should we do? Nothing, except acknowledge God's truth, which is in His Word. Scripture passages aren't to be "cherry-picked," taken out of context. The Holy Spirit serves as our personal teacher as we yearn for the Father's truth, so we mustn't worry about our ability to understand or our reading skills. We need to simply take in the full Gospel, not the hyper-grace lie. The whole Gospel encompasses tenets such as the following:

1. Many are called, but only a few are chosen (Matthew 22:14).
2. The road is narrow (Matthew 7:13).
3. We'll be hated for Jesus' name's sake (Matthew 10:22; 24:9).
4. Loving the Lord means obeying His commandments (John 14:15).

The problem today is when preachers teach only certain Scriptures and bury the ones that cause division. Preaching the entire Word of God, however, separates and cuts to the bone. Hebrews 4:12–13 says:

> For the word of God is alive and active. Sharper than any double-edged sword, it penetrates even to dividing soul and spirit, joints and marrow; it judges the thoughts and attitudes of the heart. Nothing in all creation is hidden from God's sight. Everything is uncovered and laid bare before the eyes of him to whom we must give account.

Scripture encompasses every aspect of our being, starting with God's love and ending with damnation. This is where most preachers don't want to preach the end of the story, because they want to be loved by people more than they want to honor and obey God. While it's true that God's love is so powerful that without love, there is nothing; it's also true that we can't preach that without also preaching repentance.

Eating blueberries provides our bodies with powerful antioxidants that help us fight off disease. If blueberries are all we eat, though, we'll eventually become deficient of other essential nutrients. I imagine we might also eventually turn blue! Too bad false teaching and counterfeit religion don't have a color; that would make it easier to detect the wolves in sheep's clothing. Just like an inadequate diet eventually makes a person ill, incomplete preaching makes Jesus sick.

> So, because you are lukewarm—neither hot nor cold—I am about to spit you out of my mouth. (Revelation 3:16)

It's vital to expose the enemy because Satan has many of God's children enslaved in his religious prison. God selects us to proclaim the truth and set the captives free.

That's the power of exposing the enemy.

Being a Cheerleader for Power

There's a reason football teams have cheerleaders. They motivate them to win! And when the team isn't winning, cheerleaders encourage the athletes to keep trying by boosting their spirits. We need to be cheerleaders in the realm of the supernatural, the miracle world. We need to be people of power! Many in today's church have dumbed down and even forbidden cheerleaders from being vocal, to the point of calling them names such as "people of strange fire," "children of the devil," and "deceivers." It's interesting how the religious folk called Jesus the same names. Of course, there are counterfeit gospels, miracles, and power plays, so we're addressing only the power of the True, Living God. The one test to prove authenticity is to measure it by Scripture. People who get off on a purely emotional tangent for their own benefit and don't bother to research God's written Word are a horrible detriment to His plan and can disorient, misguide, and cheerlead people straight to hell! Let's focus on God's cheerleaders—the real deal! We, as our Father's own children, must realize that in this game of eternal success, we are both players and cheerleaders. We may be one or the other at different times. God may work His power through one person, and it's the role of another to encourage and promote that. Or, God may use one person for both. The fact is, when miracles happen (all the time, all around us), we need to be aware and be prepared to boldly stand up for God. We must stop sitting in the bleachers either hiding or ridiculing the players. Now, let's get up and cheer our team on. After all, we are on the winning team!

"Give me a *P*!"

P **for Plan:** God's perfect will; His method.
O **for Omnipotence:** God's infinite, unlimited authority.
W **for Winning:** We're always on the prevailing side.
E **for Excellence:** We are always striving for and taking the higher ground.
R **for Reverence:** Respecting and giving God the glory.

Let's Discuss *P*: The Plan

From Genesis to Revelation, God reveals His plan, His method and His purpose. In doing so, He always uses His power.

God made the earth by his power, he established the world by his wisdom and by his understanding he stretched out the heavens. (Jeremiah 10:12)

God made the earth, the world, and the heavens. It all came from a place of ultimate authority, a source of infinite, all-knowing wisdom and understanding. We, as humans, will not comprehend this until we are finally in our heavenly home; however, through Scripture, we can see a glimpse of the power that our Father holds. From creation, to salvation, to destruction! This power cannot be anything but supernatural, because we walk through a natural world with temporary bodies made from dirt. However, as discussed a few chapters back, through the blood of Jesus, we are transformed into the supernatural with abilities just like our Creator. We create, save, and destroy with our thoughts, words, and actions. Since we are God's messengers, high priests, and ambassadors, we have the authority to do what Jesus did—healing, saving, and even destroying. We heal by His blood. We save by the Gospel through the Spirit, and we destroy the works of Satan when taking our position next to the Father. Jesus is the Head of the Church, and we, the Church, are the Body. Therefore, the Head can't do much without the Body because the Body has many members with many God-given gifts to accomplish the Father's work here on earth. The only way God's plan can be implemented and carried out is through the Body—us, you…and me! We possess the power, and we have the permission to use it in order to fulfill His purpose, His plan, His passion. This is to bring every soul into eternal communion with the Lord, our Father, our true God.

Let's Talk about O: Omnipotence

God's power is infinite, meaning it will never end, but let's discuss its use on the earth. When we accept Christ as the only Son of God, follow Him, and are baptized in the Spirit, we carry the badge of power, the subpoena of authority, with its forever-reaching, never-ending power right here on earth. In order to use this power, we must understand that we have the right to it. Just like a police officer's duty is to protect and serve through state-appointed power and a federal judge represents justice, we, as God's people, are appointed, anointed, and have a duty to protect, serve, and even implement justice on the enemy! We are God's A-team for the "Mission Impossible" or (if you're old enough to remember) His "Mod Squad" for miracles!

Just as God never ends, neither does the measure of His power. Jesus told us this when He said that if we have faith the size of a mustard seed, we can move mountains. Jesus said that our words could uproot a tree right out of the ground, and that the disciples would do the same miracles that He did—and even greater ones! Our power is omnipotent and continuous, and we must understand this as we face what seems to be the end of our road, whether it's a terminal illness, the loss of a loved one, the loss of freedom, emotional chaos, loneliness, or financial ruin. Just as Moses stood between the vast Red Sea and an oncoming, vicious army of Egyptians, we continuously stand between failure and success, life and death. The only thing that can deliver us is God's power, and that only happens when we trust enough to stretch out our rod of faith and wait for God to part that huge body of water in a supernatural way, defying the logical and natural. But unfortunately, most Christians stand over a small tub of water, commanding it to "part," thinking that's as good as God's power gets in these modern times. However, we must remember that God's power is as infinite, limitless, and omnipotent today as when Moses parted the sea, little David slew the giant, and Jesus extracted those dirty demons. God's power is forever, and so is our use of it!

Let's Look at *W*: What about Winning?

Too many times in church or prayer meetings, I hear more whining than winning! We need to get it through our thick religious skulls that we are to be winners—not complainers, beggars, or even asking-for-God's-will-ers! In Scripture God has already declared to us His will, yet we spend much time asking for His will, fretting about adhering to His will, and even begging for things that aren't His will! Instead, we need to be diligent in reading His Word so we can know His will. Then, just like a cop reads a criminal his or her rights, we state God's will! We serve a notice of eviction on the disease, financial hardship, or spirit of religion, and read Satan his "right to be silent." If you were playing a ballgame and could look into the future and see that your team wins, how would you play the game? You'd play with confidence, expectancy, and direction! So how much more should we play the game of salvation, eternal trophies, and forever oneness with God? Power is available to us so we can win!

Then Asa called to the Lord his God and said, "Lord, there is no one like you to help the powerless against the mighty. Help us, Lord our God, for we rely on you, and in your name we have come against this vast army. Lord, you are our God; do not let mere mortals prevail against you." (2 Chronicles 14:11)

Here we see Asa and his army facing insurmountable odds against an oncoming attack. The king reaches out to God and states four facts:

1. "Lord, there is no one like you. You are omnipotent."
2. "Lord, we are powerless without you; we rely totally on you."
3. "Lord, we are coming against this army." (Asa is stating the mission that God gave him.)
4. "Lord, you are supernatural, and you do not let the natural win over you!"

Notice the last thing Asa says is, "Lord, you do not let mere mortals win over you!" This is a man who really believes he will win in the name of the Lord!

Let's Examine *E*: Excellence

God's power should always be used in the best way and with utmost excellence. But what does this mean? Power is in many ways a tool, and a tool is used to accomplish a certain mission, just as an auto mechanic uses a set of tools to work on a car. My father always told me that the most important part of owning tools, whether for the house or the car, is keeping them clean and organized. I remember seeing my dad spending an hour or two just cleaning and organizing his tools after he finished up various projects. I asked why he did that, and he replied, "Cleaning is because I have respect for the tools, and organizing is so I will know where they all are in order to get the best use out of them. What good are tools if you don't know where they are?" This gave me my understanding of God's power. Like tools were to my earthly father, power is to my Heavenly Father. His power is to be respected and organized. But how do we do this? Well, God's power should be honored, guarded, and cherished, not thrown around like an old pair of jeans. Just as a pilot flying a 747, we have our license, but we must always get clearance to take off. Before we use the power of God, we need to always go to the Holy Spirit for clearance to initiate the Father's power.

We must also guard God's power; in other words, we are to keep it close as we would treat a very powerful weapon—concealed, but always ready to be used. Why? Have you ever gone into a restaurant and seen someone wearing a gun on his hip—open carry? It's hard not to feel different around that person, like you're always aware of him. Even though it's perfectly legal and he has the permit, he just doesn't fit in or seem quite normal. God's power is like that weapon. If we carry it around openly and blatantly, we will stick out and run the risk of appearing "holier than thou" or unapproachable. I like to have my weapon concealed. That way I can relate to almost anyone. When the enemy starts acting out, that's when I use God's power! God's people need to start cherishing this power rendered to them. What does that mean? Modern-day Christians, if they acknowledge God's power at all, many times throw it around as if Simon the sorcerer was in the room! It becomes a stage show. God forbid this! This amazing tool is to be used only for God, according to His intentions, and giving Him the glory—not some evangelist looking to be a rock star!

Why should power be organized? So that it can be used with the full force it comes from. When God's power is focused, it is most effective. Notice, Jesus Himself was always focused on His subject, whether it was healing the sick or extracting demons. Christ focused, went to the Father, and implemented the event. Sometimes He spoke, and other times He didn't. At times He did both, but with full intention and no distractions. God's power should always be used according to His Word; otherwise, it does become strange fire! I've been in some charismatic churches where the fire flew through the pews, but it wasn't God's fire. It was very strange, and did not at all witness to my spirit. Jesus said to the Pharisees, "You have two problems: first, you don't know Scripture, and second, you don't understand the power of God!" (Mark 12:24). Understanding the power of God always comes with a prerequisite: reading the Bible in order to test the Spirits. This is the only way to approach the miracles of God in the way of excellence. In order to be first class, we seek to understand the true character of the Father and know the leading of the Holy Spirit. This is only achievable by knowing Scripture. A person holding a master's degree in any field is usually looked on as qualified (even though there are many deceived theologians with degrees out the ying-yang). Someone with a degree is honored above others. That's equivalent to studying the Word of God on our own or in a corporate environment.

Let's Review R: Reverence!

At times, Jesus let those around Him know clearly that the miracle He was about to initiate was to glorify the Father. He also told the religious folks who wanted to trap Him to look at the miracles as evidence that He was indeed who He said He was—the Son! God in the flesh! He said this in efforts to have them finally bow to the True, Living God, to give the honor and respect the Father deserved. First, we pray, then we experience the miracle or the power of God, and then this is where I believe the church has really dropped the ball. We do not proclaim the miracle of God's power. It seems that we're ashamed of the miracle, fearing that the religious world will ridicule us or label us as "holy rollers" or too charismatic. Interesting how it seems that the miracles and healings our Lord performed seemed to be with little outward display of human emotion, but of course great display of spiritual emotion. His words were few, direct, and effective, and not presented as some carnival or magic show. We don't need to be outwardly emotional (even though at times the Holy Spirit can lead us there). The Spirit doesn't require emotion to display His awesome power. Remember that religion is not power, at least not power from God. Jesus told the religious people, the Pharisees, that they did not know His Father because their father was the devil! In other words, Jesus was saying that they didn't understand and accept His miracles and power because they didn't know the true source. This is very true of most of the church today. Many either condemn the power of God or misuse it by a display of works and emotion. This comes from their father, the devil, simply because their father doesn't want the true power to be revealed and used. Don't make the mistake of thinking the church that practices tradition is the only one really showing reverence to God. It is not! It is only revering tradition and not the True, Living God. Again, showing respect for God and the right to use His power is simply studying Scripture, praying for guidance from the Holy Spirit, and letting the Spirit move freely according to the will of God!

The Most Powerful Government

Daniel 7:13 says the Messiah will come on clouds from heaven and will be given the ruling power and glory over all nations so that all peoples of every language must obey Him; His power is eternal, and it will never end; His government will never fall!

This is a dream, or vision, the prophet Daniel had. He didn't understand these dreams very well at that time, but now it's easier for the people of God to see when we put on our spiritual glasses. This verse deals with the end of this age as we know it; we are coming into it—if we aren't there already. God is saying that during the midst of all the world's turmoil and nations battling nations, Christ will arrive to overcome all governments—whether a one-world government or various governments, it doesn't matter! God is the ultimate government! He will rule over all the nations so that the people of every language will obey Him. His government will never end and never fall! Throughout history (and especially now), nations have battled nations; governments have tried to rule over other governments. Nations rise, and nations fall, but not God's government, for His is the ultimate. Every language (nation) will obey His government. His power is eternal and will never fall, as this is the beginning of the new and final age, the rule of our Lord's government! When Jesus stood in front of Pilate waiting for His execution, Pilate (in all his arrogance) said to our Lord, "Don't you know I have the power?" Jesus replied, "The only power you have is the power my Father has given you." This is a truth we must understand. Even though it seems that all earthly governments have authority, the only power any government really has is what God has given them for His purpose. Notice that most big governments beat their chests and proclaim their superiority with pride and glory, but this is actually a slap in God's face, because His rule is really the ultimate government! Daniel assures us of this.

Who Is Assured to Possess the Power?

Perhaps one of the greatest cheerleaders for the kingdom of heaven is a child.

> Jesus called a little child to come to him. Jesus stood the child before the followers. Then Jesus said, "I tell you the truth. You must change and become like little children in your hearts. If you don't do this, you will never enter the kingdom of heaven." (Matthew 18:2–3, ERV)

The greatest person in the kingdom of heaven is the one who makes himself humble like this child. (Matthew 18:4, NCV)

Jesus is telling His disciples the key to getting in His kingdom: become the opposite of what they expect—a little child! When I was a boy, I remember frequently hearing this statement from adults: "Children should be seen and not heard." In other words, "Do what you're told and keep your mouth shut!" In the days when Jesus walked the earth, this attitude towards children was most likely the case. Children were loved, but they weren't significant in most matters, especially spiritual matters. But here, our Lord is turning the tables upside down on the whole spiritual world (or should I say "religious world"). In Jesus' day, the Pharisees and the scribes were leaders, revered as the "know-it-alls" of religious matters. Far be it for an insignificant child to get in their way, much less even try to exercise any degree of authority. However, this is exactly what was about to happen. Jesus says that in order to know, inherit, and use the Father's power and authority, we must become as children. You would think that mankind would have learned in these modern ages, but we still send children off to a la-la land called Sunday school and lift up the religious, educated adults as those who have some exclusive contact with the Almighty. Robes, suits, and ties, and even the latest clothing fads of the day are worn by those adults who have some gift of speaking, who are the son or daughter of someone important, or who have a great following, whether TV, radio or social media. It's all a dog and pony show unless God's people become as children; otherwise, we have nothing to say, do, or hear regarding spiritual matters.

What does it mean to become as a child? Let's take a look at the characteristics of a child, what they do and say, and how they think.

1. **Authority** – Most children understand they're under the authority of an adult. Even though they might rebel, they still know who is in charge! We are God's children and must understand

we are under complete authority to Him. Just as a child disobeys sometimes and is corrected, so are we. We disobey, we repent, and, we are corrected, all the while knowing we are under God's jurisdiction.

2. **Uninhibited (no shame)** – If you watch children, you observe that most of the time they say and act how they feel. They are brutally honest and straightforward, not even knowing (or caring) if they offend. We, as God's people, need to be uninhibited and honest instead of adhering to political correctness.

3. **Pure faith** – Children live in "believe land." Their faith is pure and undefiled by adult logic, religion, or indoctrination.

Each and every one of us comes to Jesus as a humble child. However, as He picks us up and sets us in His lap, that humble child becomes heaven's cheerleader proclaiming the true power of God.

Conclusion

I thank God for this time together with you to study and learn more about His great power in us. Only we, as the elect, have the authority to heal, cast off demons, perform miracles, and operate totally within the supernatural realm as our Lord's ambassadors, giving Him all the glory for the great authority and power bestowed upon us. As we walk in power, love, and a sound mind, let us remember that, to those who are given much, much is required. So let us march forward, rejoicing in the Lord as we take back the kingdom, one miracle at a time. Let us commit to the Father (and to one another) that we will fight the good fight and never give up until we take our last breath or our Lord returns. Though many are called and few are chosen, still, we must proclaim the Gospel as if everyone can be saved!

And remember, we've never really lived until we've found something worth dying for. Jesus said:

I am the way, the truth and the life. No one comes to the Father except through me. John 14:6

Now that is true power!